T0346925

THE POLITICAL CLASS

the POLITICAL CLASS

why it matters who our politicians are

Peter Allen

OXFORD
UNIVERSITY PRESS

OXFORD

UNIVERSITY PRESS

Great Clarendon Street, Oxford, OX2 6DP,
United Kingdom

Oxford University Press is a department of the University of Oxford.
It furthers the University's objective of excellence in research, scholarship,
and education by publishing worldwide. Oxford is a registered trade mark of
Oxford University Press in the UK and in certain other countries

© Peter Allen 2018

The moral rights of the author have been asserted

First Edition published in 2018

Impression: 1

Published in the United States of America by Oxford University Press
198 Madison Avenue, New York, NY 10016, United States of America

British Library Cataloguing in Publication Data

Data available

Library of Congress Control Number: 2017941117

ISBN 978–0–19–879597–1

Printed in Great Britain by
Clays Ltd, St Ives plc

For Marie Harrington, and in memory of John Harrington, Freda Allen, and Bill Allen.

Acknowledgements

In the documentary *Glass: A Portrait of Philip in Twelve Parts*, the composer Philip Glass discusses what it is like to finish work on a piece of music:

> At a certain point in the piece, you actually know what the piece is about. And that can happen very close to the end.[1]

As ever when you find out that someone else shares in what you thought was a dreadful behavioural disorder that was by some metaphysical prank embarrassingly unique to yourself, I was delighted to hear him say this. I have felt like this about everything I have ever written, and this book was no exception. Now it is finished, I feel like I know what it is about. In the spirit of the book, the diverse perspectives of a lot of people helped me get there, and they all deserve thanks.

Many colleagues and correspondents have discussed the ideas of this book with me, or contributed in some other way, often without being aware that they were doing so. I would like to thank Rosie Campbell, Sarah Childs, Phil Cowley, Will Jennings, Mike Kenny, Charlie Lees, Joni Lovenduski, Jon Mellon, Rainbow Murray, and Nick Startin.

Special thanks are owed to Paul Cairney, with whom I wrote a paper on the subject of the political class; to Dave Cutts, who has spoken to me about this subject and many others for many hours; and to Dai Moon, who helped me figure out why I was confusing myself in Chapter 4 and gave comments on other sections.

At Oxford University Press, thanks to Matthew Cotton, Martha Cunneen, Gayathri Manoharan, Luciana O'Flaherty, and Kizzy Taylor-Richelieu for seeing the book safely from idea through to manuscript. Thanks also to Neil Morris for his careful editing of the text.

Thanks to Freedom for Mac for giving me exactly that.

1. *Glass: A Portrait of Philip in Twelve Parts*, directed by Scott Hicks, 2007.

Outside of work, my friends and family have helped the book along in various ways. Thanks to my parents, Tony and Angela, and to Fiona, my sister, who have always given me the ideal mix of space and interest that I needed to get on with whatever I was doing. Also for this, and for everything else, I would like to thank Rebecca: first reader, gentle critic, and the most interesting person I know.

Finally, I dedicate this book to my grandmother Marie Harrington, also known to me as Momma, among other things. She has been the biggest supporter of this book since I first mentioned that I might write it, and her continued interest in it has been a great source of encouragement. I also dedicate the book to the memory of my other, sadly late, grandparents—Bill Allen (Papa), Freda Allen (Nan), and John Harrington (Grandad). Getting to know my grandparents so well has been a great privilege and I hope that this book displays the same open-mindedness with which I have witnessed them live their lives.

Peter Allen

January 2017, Bristol

Contents

List of figures

List of tables

Introduction

You and I will likely have little to no direct role in crafting the laws that shape our lives and the lives of the people we know during our time on Earth. Our expertise, such as it is, will go unused, our thoughts and ideas unacted on, and our individual voices unheard in those ancient chambers of power from where we are all governed.[1] We may write to our representatives, put our names to petitions, and turn out to vote for others, but the chances are that we will never be there in the room, making decisions and writing the rules under which we live. If you are a woman, are from an ethnic minority, are working class, or do not hold a degree, the likelihood of your ever holding a position of political power is even lower than mine, a white middle-class male university lecturer. If you do not feel a particular affinity with one of the main political parties in existence right now, you might as well forget the idea of holding political office altogether. Instead of casting the net wide in search of our political leaders, we continue to elect politicians who are similar to one another and unlike everyone else.

I can imagine that many people might think that this is simply not an issue worthy of our concern. Politicians are often of a kind but, even if they are not perfect in this regard, they are probably better suited to the job than others overall. I used to hold something like this complacent view, perhaps because I was the kind of person who looked like they might end up as a politician—I had studied politics at university, I avidly consumed political coverage in the media, and I was involved in a political party. But as each year passed, I realized that I was slowly moving away from being that kind of person. With each year that I didn't intensify my political activity, and as my tolerance for watching political coverage withered to almost zero, it dawned on me that although I was still much closer than most to having a chance of being directly involved in political decision-making, the chance that I could run for political office was rapidly diminishing. This fact wasn't especially distressing to me on a personal level, but it did get me thinking. Is this just, that most of us can say for sure, right now, that we will never be directly involved in making political decisions? More than this, is it a sensible use of all the talents that we see at work around us every single day as we move through the world? The fact that so few of us must ever have even the vaguest of thoughts about one day holding political office in the first place, let alone that those of us who do have such a small window of opportunity to act on them, struck me as not a good thing. It still does.

In the years since I had this realization, I have dedicated a lot of my professional life to exploring the questions it threw up. If most of us do not become politicians, who does? Does it matter either way? My feelings about how to respond to the problem are best characterized as those of acute ambivalence. On the one hand, I know from direct experience that politicians are not all bad. In my professional and personal life I meet plenty of them, and I've campaigned for a few who are decent people driven by a straightforward desire to do good. On the other hand, I am increasingly despondent about the state of political institutions and political culture in modern Britain. Although Members of Parliament have become more representative of the wider population in certain senses, with more women and ethnic-minority MPs sitting in Parliament than ever before, the distance between those of us who are interested and involved in formal politics and those who are not seems to be growing. Coverage and discussion of politics in the media and academia feel utterly inadequate for the task of changing this or of even facilitating a discussion about it. More often than not, it exacerbates the problem. So, what to do? For all the times I have had my head turned for a few days or longer by some argument or an interesting refutation, I have always come back to the same thought: that the kind of people our politicians are, and what they bring to political life, matters.

The view I hold is simple. In terms of what can, and should, be changed about British politics right now, the question of composition needs to be top of the agenda. I think that dealing with this issue is maybe the single most influential thing we could do to break the cycle of anti-political thinking we appear to be stuck in and to rejuvenate public interest and investment in the political process. Of course, there are other changes that could be made, such as reforming the procedures of the House of Commons, changing the electoral system, helping the public to somehow understand democracy better, or promoting civic engagement in schools and universities.[2] These might make some difference. But I believe changing who our politicians are will make a bigger one, and in this book I want to convince you of the same.

The Problem of the Political Class

Right now, the British people do not like their politicians.[3] Although it is hard to say precisely how this dislike compares with the disdain shown to elected officials in the past, it is even harder to deny the pervading sense that the shouts of complaint are either growing in number, in noise, or both. A common target of these attacks is not a singularly unpopular politician but rather the so-called 'political class', a group supposedly led by career politicians who collectively feed from the trough of publicly funded political institutions, who fail to represent the public at large, and who are a noxious mix of self-serving indifference. This has fed into a broader feeling of disconnect between politicians and the people, and to what has been seen as a mutual withdrawal by both: politicians withdrawing into the protected space of political institutions filled with others like themselves, and the people withdrawing from the political process altogether.[4*]

The sustained prominence of this question of who our politicians are suggests that the public have also intuited a mislaying of fairness, effectiveness, or both. In particular, the question of who our politicians are has gained a foothold in the public debate about the ills of the British political system. The members of our political class, we are told, are all the same—venal career and professional politicians looking out for themselves. As Nigel Farage has put it, 'We have a career political class. You know the people I'm talking about. They all go to the same schools. They all go to Oxford. They all study PPE. They leave at 22 and get a job as a researcher for one of the parties and then become MPs at age 27 or 28.' For Farage, this is equivalent to these people never having 'done a day of work in their lives'.[5] They are a metropolitan elite. They are Europhiles. They are politically correct. And so on. Combined, the popular indictment of the political class is fairly incriminating.

The case against the political class rests mainly on two assertions. First, the political class does not represent the diversity of all kinds present in the wider public. Second, this situation is in someway unfair, unjust, and may also be having a negative effect on the quality of political decisions being made by our elected representatives.

These are not charges without at least some foundation in reality. Academic accounts of elite politicians have focused on changes in the nature of British political life that might have resulted in the formation of such a self-sustaining and secure group of people at the top of politics and the resultant composition of our political institutions.[6] For example, we know that the introduction and growth of salaries for MPs during the twentieth century had the effect of diversifying the social-class backgrounds of those elected to the House of Commons, but also led to increased parliamentary tenures. Similarly, the professionalization of the legislature as a whole has caused the development of a parasitic industry of political staffers within Parliament itself, political parties, and a plethora of think tanks and lobbying firms based in or around Westminster. In turn, this now means that an increasing number of MPs work in these kinds of jobs prior to becoming elected politicians. In effect, a not insignificant number will never earn a living by working outside of politics before entering the House of Commons. If representative democracy is at least in part about distilling the voices of the many into a smaller group of people who can transmit these into the political sphere, can it function if the people acting as transmitters are increasingly similar to one another and decreasingly like everyone else?

The general reaction to this issue of the political class has been two-fold. On the one hand some, including academics, have rushed to the defence of politics and our politicians as a whole. The general argument put forward has been that yes, there are certain things that could be changed, but overall things are better than they have been in the past, or might be in future should anything hasty be undertaken in the name of reform. On the other hand, angry polemics have been written that assume, and seek to demonstrate, the very worst about our politicians.

Professional students of politics, like political scientists or political theorists, have a tendency to talk a lot about how structure and agency affect political outcomes.[7] Agency can be seen as essentially the things that people either do or do not do. On an agency-focused reading of political events, we assume that people either do or do not do things and that the social world that we live in is to a large extent the result of these actions or non-actions. Conversely, structure is thought of as those underlying forces within society and the world that bring about the social sphere in which we exist. These would be things like broad economic development over time. On this sort of reading, human actions (that is, agency) do not have so much of an effect.

The dominant account of the political-class problem focuses heavily on agency, seeing politicians as looking out for themselves as members of a selfish cartel. I'm not convinced that this is the whole story. Instead, I want to look beyond this explanation and instead consider more structural explanations. In particular, the aim is to offer some sense of how structure might not necessarily determine actions, but maintain that actions simply have to be influenced in some way by the context in which they exist.

In doing so, I want to highlight how in some ways it shouldn't be that surprising that the political class looks the way it does right now given the societal conditions in which it exists and which have shaped it. I will also suggest that it is perhaps equally to be expected that many of our politicians consequently end up thinking the same kinds of things about politics given the structures and institutions in which they exist and the process by which they gain access to these positions. In short, I am far from convinced that individual politicians can be held accountable for the development of the status quo. However, they *can* be held accountable for sustaining it, and they should be pushed to change it.

Democracy, Representation, Inclusion, and Equality

Britain is widely proclaimed as a democracy, and democracy can be defined at root as the rule of the people.[8] Starting from this simple idea, some arguments against the political class rest on the assumption that a wholesale move to direct democracy, involving all citizens participating in either smaller-scale legislative chambers or in rolling referendums on all issues, would be more democratic than a representative system which is not itself considered truly democratic. For those supporting such arguments, it is the *representation* part of representative democracy itself that is the issue, not any particular pattern of representation within that framework. For them, democracy requires the involvement of all of us in political decision-making all of the time.

I do not endorse this position, but I freely admit that the arguments against, for example, direct democracy can often be question-begging— 'the country is too big/politics too complicated to have a direct democracy so we should not have a direct democracy'. Having said that, questions of scale cannot simply be dismissed as too boring to care about. The UK population is roughly 65 million people, many of whom who live in densely populated urban areas. It is not clear how smaller-scale legislative chambers consisting of all citizens might actually function in this context, one where the population is not evenly spread across all available (and hospitable) space. Even if we took a different approach and said that direct democratic chambers would be in place for every 5,000 people (still a large number), for example, this might mean that some rural areas stretching hundreds of miles would have one legislative body, whilst the London Borough of Tower Hamlets, with an area of 8 square miles, would have 57. Crucially, none of these areas would exist in a vacuum, so it would be quite likely that representatives from each would need to be sent to some higher-level body to discuss issues affecting all of them in any case. Readers will recognize in this idea the logic behind supranational governance initiatives involving multiple states or, more obviously, a national representative assembly. Thinking instead in terms of a series of rolling referendums, these concerns seem to matter less, though there would be a number of preliminary decisions required in order to establish when a referendum would be required, if this would be in lieu of or in addition to a representative assembly, whether turnout would be compelled or voluntary, and so on. These arguments can feel quite tedious to those in favour of small-scale direct democracy, based as they are on rather dull practicalities, but they are nonetheless persuasive. For those of us living in polities of this size, scale seems to be a fairly inescapable constraint on our thinking about political reform.

More importantly, though, it is simply not the case that democracy requires this kind of direct involvement of all of us, all of the time, to live up to its name. Many have defended representative democracy against this view, arguing that its reputation as the poor relation of the truly democratic direct form of democracy is not only unfair, but also unwarranted.[9] This falsehood that representation and democracy are not able to produce 'genuine' democracy is referred to by the political theorist Nadia Urbinati as the 'incompatibility doctrine'.[10] This claim of incompatibility rests on the notion that democracy can only happen when all concerned individuals are directly there making the decisions and exercising their sovereign will. Thus, the way that representative government is enacted via election is exclusionary by definition and therefore undemocratic. Some have argued against the incompatibility doctrine and claimed that 'representative democracy is neither an oxymoron, nor merely a pragmatic alternative for something we, modern citizens, can no longer have'.[11] As another political theorist, David Plotke, puts it, '[T]he opposite of representation is not participation. The opposite of representation is exclusion. And the opposite of participation is abstention.'[12] Representative democracy can thus be democratic under certain circumstances, and more or less democratic based on specific factors, especially *who* the representatives actually are. Right now, the British political class is comprised of a relatively uniform group of people—it is not diverse. Some do not see this lack of diversity as a problem and even defend it in various ways, while others argue strongly that we need more diversity among politicians for a multitude of reasons relating to representation, equality, and inclusion. I will briefly address these ideas in turn.

This first idea of *political representation* is one of the most contested concepts in political studies. For the purposes of what is covered in this book, I think about political representation as a process and system by and in which the overall population selects a smaller group of people to attend to the functions of the formal institutions of the political system on their behalf. In some sense, it is a way of distilling the broader populace into a concentrated version of itself. The two kinds of political representation I discuss a lot in what follows are *descriptive representation* and *substantive representation*. Descriptive representation refers to the presence of certain types of people in given places or institutions. So, for example, if I went to a branch of a high-street optician, it is likely that the descriptive representation of people who wear glasses is going to be high. Conversely, the descriptive representation of individuals from ethnic minorities in the House of Commons is low. Substantive representation is perhaps more familiar and refers to the representation of the political interests, broadly defined, of different groups of society. If a law was passed that made eye tests and new pairs of glasses free, this law could convincingly be considered as substantively representative of the interests of glasses wearers. On the other hand, a law that limited women's access to abortion further than is currently the case might be considered to not substantively represent the interests of women, though this relationship is complicated, particularly in this case.[13] Bringing these thoughts on representation together, having a representative system means that, by default, a smaller group than the entire population is involved in the workings of politics at any given time. In the process of doing this, we rely on a certain configuration of descriptive representation in an attempt to bring about some kind of substantive representation for the wider group. Traditionally, as I will demonstrate, certain powerful groups of society have been descriptively over-represented. Jeffrey Green refers to this characteristic of all representative systems as that of 'remove':

...the ordinary citizen's perceived sense of occupying the periphery of power – of lacking the notoriety, influence, and wealth that would make it possible to operate in politics as an *individual* whose decisions have a direct bearing on political events – and at the same time knowing that there are others who do not face this same lack.[14]

In a representative system, an overwhelming majority of us will be absent from positions of political power, while a small number will occupy them. This is a fixed point within any such system and cannot be avoided. We might think of this as an inevitable characteristic. However, the descriptive character of who actually comprises the smaller group is not inevitable at all. As such, the truly interesting question is that of how inclusion and its opposite are justified—on what grounds are some included among the politically powerful and others not?

This brings us to the concept of *inclusion*. I think of inclusion, following others who have written about it in the past, as the ability of those affected by political decisions to be included in the decision-making process and to influence political outcomes.[15] So, building on the above, exactly *what kinds of people* are counted among those holding positions of political power? How diverse a group are the politicians who sit in Parliament, in all senses of the word? Right now, as I will show in greater detail in the next chapter, British politics does not perform well on this count.

What of equality? Although equality is often considered exclusively in economic terms, I want to focus also on how equality relates to involvement in politics. The notion of *political equality* that I use in this book is closely related to the idea of inclusion. For my purposes, equality would be something along the lines of a situation in which individuals bearing characteristics of various kinds did not appear to be systematically excluded from the holding of political office. My argument in this book is that various structural inequalities in society are the primary cause of the kind of non-inclusive, and fundamentally unrepresentative and non-diverse, political class that we have in Britain today. It is thanks to these various mounting and intersecting inequalities that our politics is the way it is—and, more particularly, why it is dominated by the people it is. For example, socio-economic, educational, gender, class, racial, and geographic inequality, to name but a few, all affect how inclusive politics is, and ultimately how well our representative democracy lives up to its name.

Diversity

The trio of concepts discussed above are united by their relationship to the further concept of diversity. Throughout the book I will discuss diversity of all kinds. This includes the kind of diversity we most often think of when we hear the word—for example, in terms of gender, ethnicity, age, which can be referred to as *identity diversity*—and also a different kind of diversity known as *cognitive diversity*. Scott Page identifies four key components to cognitive diversity. Diverse perspectives (seeing problems and situations differently), diverse interpretations (different ways of categorizing things), diverse heuristics (different methods of problem-solving), and diverse predictive models (different understandings of causal relationships in the world). Combined, these structure the way that individuals approach instances of both problem-solving and prediction in the world.

There is a parallel of sorts between the descriptive and substantive representation and identity and cognitive diversity, respectively. In both cases, although diversity in the former (descriptive representation and identity diversity) does not always result in systematic differences along the same lines in the latter (substantive representation and cognitive diversity), the link between the two seems to hold, as I discuss further in Chapter 3. Consequently, if we are looking to gain access to a wider range of opinion in political life, we could do worse than having a wider range of people in descriptive terms—getting a more identity-diverse group of people into politics seems to lead to greater cognitive diversity.

A Summary of the Main Argument

As the above suggests, representative democratic political systems walk a difficult path, seeking to combine principles of equality, diversity, and inclusion with a structure that, by definition, has to exclude some. They seek, all of this considered, to be representative nonetheless.

At the core of the issue of the political class is a failing of this function of representation. People feel that politicians do not represent them. They think this is unfair and that it leaves them standing in a position of inequality relative to those who are perceived to be represented well. These feelings have arisen at least in part thanks to us having a political system that does not effectively include a broad enough range of people in its workings. It certainly is undeniable that, to use the term defined above, the political class is not descriptively representative of the British people as a whole.

This failing of representation is the result of broader social and political inequality. Crucially, the selection of those who are among the politically powerful takes place not only on the grounds of ideology or wider political reasons, or indeed by reason of supposed merit, but on the grounds of the kinds of inequality that systematically limit the opportunity of many of the population to hold and exercise real political influence. Quite simply, the odds are set against most people ever holding positions of political power owing to circumstances that are, have been, and always will be beyond their control.

One might think this is simple enough to solve—just get a more diverse group of people into politics. This does, indeed, sound simple, but the notion that this lack of diversity is a bad thing at all is heavily contested. Resistance to bringing a wider range of people into positions of political decision-making often comes from those who worry that doing so would reduce the quality of politicians present in the institution and thus the quality of the decisions it makes. This is what I call the *epistemic defence* of the political class, since it focuses on the knowledge held by that non-diverse group. The thought is that although the political class, as it currently is, lacks diversity, this can be justified by its members' superiority as political operatives and their possession of superior political knowledge. This defence intentionally casts politics as an exclusive activity, one that should be dominated by a certain kind of person—a person with a long-standing and sustained engagement with formal political organizations or institutions and with a high level of demonstrable political knowledge. Of course, such traits are most likely to be found among those groups who already dominate political institutions in terms of socio-economic status, ethnicity, and sex, among others. As a result, the exclusionary tendencies of the epistemic defence lock in the lack of identity diversity that is already a feature of the political class.

The epistemic defence of the political class also tends to come packaged with a dose of what I refer to as *epistemic snobbery*, whereby people who do not meet the above criteria of political inclusion are not seen as worthy participants or contributors in political discussions, or whereby their political opinions are devalued in some way.[16] This policing of what counts as a political contribution and of who can make it is simultaneously reflective of the homogeneity of the political class and aids in the perpetuation of it. I discuss this further in the final chapter, particularly the way in which, even as we gratefully see certain barriers to inclusion weaken, like those that previously almost entirely excluded women and ethnic minorities from political office, others rise and strengthen in their stead.

However, it is in my view not the most robust of defences, and in the first instance relies on a number of tendentious assumptions regarding the question of what politics actually is. I mount two main arguments against this epistemic defence. The first is an intrinsic defence of democratic inclusion, which argues that having a non-diverse political class violates the tenets of political equality that lie at the heart of any democratic system worthy of the name.

A second, related element is the sense that by limiting the kinds of people who tend to become politicians, we might be harming the instrumental effectiveness and desirability of the political outcomes they produce. Work by Scott Page and his colleague Lu Hong has shown that increasing the cognitive diversity of a pool of decision makers by introducing a more diverse range of perspectives has an overwhelmingly positive effect on the group's collective problem-solving ability. How do you increase cognitive diversity among political decision makers? By making political institutions inclusive.

Ultimately, I do not fully endorse this instrumental case against the current political class, partly owing to the assumptions about politics it also requires us to make. Not only is an intrinsic defence of democracy perhaps more convincing, it is also incredibly hard to refute. My contention is that those who broadly defend the current situation in the UK and other advanced democracies, whereby the political class is dominated by a relatively homogeneous group of people, are putting themselves in a pretty difficult position. At the very least, even if you do not fully support my suggested fixes when you put this book down, I think you will be hard pressed to deny that there is a problem here.

Historically, people have been wary of making the intrinsic and instrumental arguments together, fearing that straying beyond a principled case for a diverse political class somehow dilutes its power, or leaves claims for justice open to qualification or quibbling about the outcome they are now thought to be conditional on. To be clear, I think the intrinsic argument is the most powerful argument in favour of diversity in politics but, as I will go on to discuss later, I think we already tend to sneak instrumental arguments in via the back door as it is. This, plus the fact that these arguments increasingly make themselves hard to ignore, is why I include them.

Crucially this book is not about blaming individual politicians or cataloguing their supposed sins at length. As satisfying as this exercise may be, it does not really get us anywhere, not to mention the fact that a wagging finger in the form of a book would be rather trying to read. A focus on increasing diversity gives a clear target to aim at—making the system more inclusive of a wider range of people—which in turn allows us to devote our energies to a smaller number of potential changes that can actually be made. For example, if inclusion is our goal, we should draw attention to the points at which access to politics is limited for certain groups, namely the role that political parties play in recruiting potential politicians or the inhibiting cost of mounting a candidacy for political office.

Before I proceed, I want to be clear about what I am *not* advocating in what follows. Put simply, I am not advocating the assumption, or more often the assertion, that only people from social group X have the authority (presumably moral or otherwise) to speak on behalf of that group or about the lived experience of that group, broadly defined. For example, a typical case of this might be that a white woman does not have the authority to speak about the lived experiences of African-American women, or that a gay single woman in her twenties cannot, and should not, speak about the life of a 77-year-old heterosexual married man.[17]

This is a thorny issue, and one that has gained much journalistic attention in recent years. A major question in play in these debates is whether people should have the right to speak about others who are unlike themselves in a relevant way. It seems fairly apparent to me that the answer to this should be 'yes, they can'. Opponents often correctly point out that this is a sound position to hold in theory, but that in practice individuals do not all have an equal voice or an equal ability to be heard. This is true, and is at least part of the reason that I advocate the position I do in this book. Greater diversity among those who sit in these powerful political positions, and in who has such a voice, will help reduce the impact of differential power relations. This being said, it is also true that equalizing political participation does sometimes require the exclusion, albeit temporary, of certain powerful interests or groups.

However, the point here is not that an all-male legislature, for example, simply cannot and never could represent the interests of women—In theory, I think it could under strict conditions involving large-scale consultation exercises, a major role for aggregative pressure groups, and so on. Instead, the contention is that this would be undemocratic and thus undesirable for reasons not necessarily related to the political outcomes it resulted in. Committing to bringing about a greater pluralism in those involved in our politics is about making a commitment to the way in which we want politics to function. It is not about a substantive commitment to seek certain kinds of political outcomes. It is a commitment to representative democracy as a form of political practice, and a political practice that currently systematically excludes much of the population cannot be considered to be representative and, consequently, sufficiently democratic.

Why You Should Care

Why should you or anyone else care about this? It is a fair question. As Churchill famously said, 'No one pretends that democracy is perfect or all-wise. Indeed, it has been said that democracy is the worst form of government except all those other forms that have been tried from time to time.' I expect that some readers' response to my argument will be Churchill-like. Many people feel, perhaps rightly, that there is no urgency required on this matter. Although this may seem to be the case, there are fundamental changes taking place in British society that can be linked back to these core issues of diversity, representation, inclusion, and equality. To start with, we know that Britain is becoming a more unequal society overall, with the gap between rich and poor growing year-on-year. The painstaking work of economist Thomas Piketty has shown how inherited wealth and other capital earned not via wages but gained from initial existing investments are making the UK and other Western countries increasingly unequal.[18] In other words, the amount of money that individuals actually earn will make little difference to their overall relative wealth: those who started with more money are going to continue to have more money regardless of how much they earn.[19] This is a result of the concentrated accumulation of assets such as property by wealthier individuals. In the case of housing, this has caused an ever increasing number of younger people and families to rent their accommodation on a month-to-month basis. It has made their lives more precarious. This might not be such a contentious issue if the British private rental sector was regulated as closely as those of our European neighbours, but the current system is favourable for landlords. Despite a creeping sense of crisis in the rental market as a whole, legislative progress in actually bringing in a new regulatory framework has been slow. Perhaps not coincidentally, 153 MPs were listed as landlords on official parliamentary records in 2015.[20]

What we are seeing overall is a concentration of economic capital, and all the security and opportunity that this carries with it, in the hands of a decreasing number of people. Concurrently, we are seeing a broad withdrawal from the political process by a growing number of people.[21] I am not claiming that these two phenomena are definitely linked—that kind of certainty is not available to us as social scientists. However, it stands to reason that they might be connected in important ways. For example, recent research by Oliver Heath suggests that as the number of working-class election candidates declines, so does the participation of working-class voters.[22]

We also know that those with greater economic capital are more likely to be politically involved. You could say that their economic advantage leaves them better placed to make use of their political rights. As Jeffrey Green puts it, 'Insofar as wealth generates both an incentive to participate and a means of doing so, the wealthy—and perhaps the very wealthy—will have a disproportionate advantage in politics.'[23] We also know that young people are less likely to vote but appear to be suffering the effects of political decisions made in the name of austerity more than any other social group.[24] I am not saying that if a broader range of people is involved in politics the outcomes will definitely be different or somehow kinder to everyone who currently does badly out of political decisions. I am not convinced that they would be. But having a broader range of people should allow for the airing of a broader range of views, and available evidence suggests that the views of those who are not particularly wealthy are different from those who are. As Geoff Evans and James Tilley write, 'To put it bluntly, poor people want the state to be redistributive and protectionist, and rich people don't.'[25] If one group is present when laws are made, and another is not, this will matter.

This book has four chapters plus this introduction and a conclusion. In Chapter 1, I sketch the contours of the political-class debate. The general argument is that the political class is considered to be non-diverse, this pattern described by something I refer to as the political-class narrative. The narrative has three strands. The first focuses on characteristic homogeneity, the second attitudinal homogeneity, and the third behavioural homogeneity. The chapter lays out examples of each, but only offers solid evidence to support the first strand, that which focuses on the characteristics of members of the political class. Regardless, and to be clear, this is evidence in support of at least part of the overall criticisms we hear of the political class.

Chapter 2 outlines a possible defence of the inequalities inherent in the status quo, essentially putting forward the reasons why the unrepresentativeness shown in the previous chapter might not be of concern. The defence hinges on claims made about both the nature of politics, mainly that it is a domain requiring effective problem-solving ahead of broader representation, and the ignorance of the electorate at large. In short, it is an *epistemic* defence of the political class based on the claim that the smaller, non-diverse group of politicians we have will know better than the masses. It also offers a defence by explanation, showing how various larger social and economic forces may have led us to the door of a homogeneous political class. Furthermore, the good intentions of politicians and the value of a representative system as a whole are defended.

Chapter 3 turns the tables and offers the case against the inequality at the core of the current political class. The chapter opens with an intrinsic defence of diversity in the political class, arguing that it is a core tenet of the expectation of political equality at the heart of democracy. Moving on, the chapter then considers various problems with the way that politics, and political knowledge, are conceived in the defence offered in Chapter 2 before discussing novel research across various fields that suggests the 'dumb many' of the electorate might not be so dumb after all. Indeed, an instrumental argument in favour of diversity is offered that speculates how a diverse political class might make better decisions than the current limited one. Although the intrinsic defence is ultimately endorsed ahead of the instrumental defence, it nonetheless offers food for thought.

Chapter 4 assumes, hopefully not too optimistically, that by this point most readers are convinced that the lack of diversity within the political class is problematic. This established, attention now turns to what might be done to ameliorate this malady. There is a broad split in the chapter between those reforms that might be made while keeping a system of election by which we select our political representatives and those reforms that do not include this, namely the adoption of a system of randomly selecting members of the political class. The former reforms primarily focus on the role that political parties and political institutions can play in shifting existing patterns of supply and demand in order to diversify the pool of prospective, selected, and elected candidates for office. This is tightly bound to the intrinsic defence of diversity offered previously. The latter reforms relate more closely to the instrumental or epistemic argument in favour of diversity. In the end, I do not express loyalty to either proposal in particular, but rather use them to illustrate the potential work that might be ahead should the issue be taken seriously by policymakers and other political actors.

The book's conclusion summarizes the core arguments before offering some wider reflections and prescriptions on how each of us can do our part to prevent further divisions developing between the politically involved and everyone else, with a particular focus on the professional political commentariat.

A final note before we proceed. There is a temptation when writing academically to make clear exactly how much material the author has read and how complicated what they do actually is. This often comes at the expense of readability and clarity. I suspect this behaviour stems from a fear of being caught out, a fear of being told you are wrong that far outstrips the fear of not writing well. As Steven Pinker puts it, being an academic trying to write for a general audience often sees you 'walk on eggshells, terrified that you'll let slip the horrible truth that you're not rigorous, sophisticated, and cultivated enough to belong to the club'.[26] In writing this book, I have done my best to avoid this, and I generally avoid listing all possible counterarguments or slight variations on a given theme. Some academic readers might consider some sections to be too brief or lacking in nuance, but I hope that for most readers these omissions will go unnoticed.

This book is about how who our politicians are is affecting the kind of society we live in. It is about why the way this is right now might be inevitable, why it might not be, and how we could change it. The first task of the book is to be more specific about how our political institutions are currently not inclusive or representative in terms of who is present within them. This is the work of Chapter 1.

1

Who or What is the Political Class?

Writing in 2009, the political scientist Michael Kenny asked:

Has a political elite emerged on top of British society? Is politics dominated by a narrow caste of political 'professionals'? Are politicians preponderantly corrupt and self-serving? And, has a populist desire to follow, not lead, public opinion resulted in the dangerous weakening of the principle of representation that underpins the British parliamentary model?[1]

These questions are indicative of the kinds of issues that circle the political class and addressing these, and others like them, is the work of this book. To answer them properly, however, we first need to understand exactly what we mean when we talk about the political class. When trying to assess or account for any social phenomenon, a good starting point is to come up with an answer to the question of how best to define it.[2] In almost all cases this is not a simple exercise. Defining the term 'political class' is no exception, and I do not hope to make any final pronouncements on the issue here. Instead, I want to give readers a sense of how the term has been employed in the past, and provide some structure to what can often seem like a chaotically varied usage of the term.

My approach is to separate out the object of the political class itself and what I refer to as the 'political-class narrative'. The latter has three strands, all of which focus on the lack of diversity in the political class in some way. The first focuses on the characteristics of the political class, the second on its members' attitudes, and the third on their behaviour. I provide multiple examples of the complaints in each strand of the narrative, and offer some judgement on whether there is evidence to support the general thrust of the accusations. Overall, the claims of uniformity in the behaviour and attitudes of the political class are often far-fetched and unsubstantiated, although it is perhaps most accurate to say that they apply to different members of the political class to a greater or lesser extent. In contrast, the criticisms regarding the lack of characteristic or identity diversity within the political class are largely accurate. As such, this is the most robust element of the political-class narrative, and the evidence supporting it is convincing.

The idea of a ruling, or political, class is not new. Since the Italian sociologist Gaetano Mosca popularized the idea in the 1930s, the thought that there is a societal elite who hold the reins of political power has shown itself to be a persistent one.[3] Various terms have acted as crystallizations of concern about this concentration of influence—the political class, the ruling class, the establishment, and I imagine many others that I am unaware of. In this chapter, and this book, I focus on the idea of the political class, and in particular on contemporary discussion of it over the last twenty years or so. This should not be taken as offering anything near a comprehensive account of the history of the idea, but rather as offering context and empirical evidence to ground what follows after.

A major distinction between different uses of the term 'political class' is that in some cases the term is used descriptively to denote some group of individuals and in others is instead used in a way that carries normative weight, generally of a negative kind. Here lies a broader conceptual question about where we draw a line that separates the occupations that make people 'count' as part of the political class. When it comes to identifying individual members of the political class, there often seems to be the assumption that 'we know it when we see it'. This is in spite of the fact that it is difficult to find a settled-upon classification of *exactly* who or what we are talking about. Some, for example, prefer a broader definition that encompasses people involved at all levels of politics, all over the country. Uwe Jun, a proponent of this view, writes:

While MPs are at the center of the political class, the group also includes the growing numbers of political consultants, political advisors to ministers, research assistants to MPs, as well as the staff at party headquarters, in the House of Commons, and in policy research institutes working for the parties. To this list should also be added lobbyists working for interest organizations. On the regional and local level the class includes the members of newly established legislatures and assemblies, their staff and political advisors, and the growing number of professional councillors and members of local government.[4]

This is a lot of people, many of whom can safely be judged as not guilty of the supposed myriad sins of the political class that we often hear discussed. Jun, however, is not alone in casting a wide net when deciding who is in and who is out. In his 2014 book *The Establishment*, the political commentator Owen Jones identifies a group of people that he refers to as 'the Establishment' who hold both great power and wealth in contemporary Britain.[5] They are, he writes, 'mostly unelected and unaccountable people who really do rule the roost, not only through their shared wealth and power, but because of the ideas and mentalities that govern their behaviour'.[6] I will return to Jones's classification below, but a brief glimpse at the chapter headings in his book shows that he includes MPs, the police, the media, big business, and the financial City of London in his classification of the Establishment. Jones is not specifically discussing the political class as such, but many of his criticisms about leading politicians sit well as part of the conversation I am interested in here.

So, where should the line be drawn? Which occupations allow the holder of them to count as a member of the political class, and which do not? Inherent in any definition game are multiple trade-offs. Consistent with the long-standing tradition of elite theory within the discipline of political studies, I am not opposed to thinking about there being an overarching elite or establishment class in this way. Indeed, as I will demonstrate later on, the way I think about the question of the political class, and political power, is one in which membership of a political elite is almost intractably bound up with membership of other privileged societal groups which, when combined, might be seen to comprise exactly this kind of elite class or sodality. To be clear, I think that process by which the political class has become what I will show it to be is built on numerous inequalities in wider society—the fact that your age, sex, ethnicity, and socio-economic status, to name but a few things, to an overwhelming degree structure your opportunities to exert political influence. This idea, that our experience of the political world is inescapably tarnished in this way, even in countries that are widely held as archetypal liberal democracies, has been described by the philosopher Jeffrey Green as 'the shadow of unfairness'.[7] I will discuss this idea more as I move along, primarily in the conclusion, but it underlies much of what I say.

All told, I do agree with Jones, Jun, and others who have written on the topic that this is true of a wider range of positions of political power and influence than I can do justice to in this book. I think it is safe to assume that the problems I identify as afflicting our elected political class are probably true of the political journalists who report on them, those working in the think tanks that feed them policy ideas, and many others who hold a less prominent but no less powerful role in making our political weather.

Definitions are, to a point, somewhat arbitrary. If it looks like a duck and quacks like a duck, and so on and so on. But we should also be keenly aware that, regardless of their arbitrariness, definitions go out in to the world and do the bidding of those who encourage their usage. So, we might think that the print or broadcast media will encourage a definition of the political class that excludes them from it, as might Nigel Farage, or Donald Trump. Or, more specifically, certain political parties, media outlets, or advocacy organizations will seek to locate themselves outside the supposed poisoned well.

At any rate, my preference is for a relatively minimal definition that focuses attention on national-level politicians sitting in Westminster, though, as noted, I do not see an overarching imposition of a set definition as something without which we cannot proceed.[8] There are three main reasons why I prefer a limited classification here. First, elected politicians have a representative function that unelected occupations simply do not have. There is something unique about being an elected representative that is just not there for other jobs that are also political but do not involve election or a representative function of any kind. Second, MPs are based in Westminster, where power still, for the most part, resides in UK politics.[9] Part of the political-class narrative focuses on the idea of a 'Westminster village', and it is undeniably different to be an MP at Westminster as opposed to a local councillor in Gateshead. I think this difference matters. Third, nearly all MPs have clearly stated and acted on a public preference for one political party at the expense of the others. Given the importance of party in British political life, this too makes a difference. Being in a party ingratiates individuals into networks they would otherwise not have access to, networks that might aid the sustainability and longevity of their political career.

Thus I favour making a distinction between the political class as a term that simply marks out a group of people that could probably be identified in any political system in the world, and what I call the political-class narrative, which is the multifaceted discussion that surrounds such a group. This kind of narrative could also probably be found anywhere that one wished to look for it.[10] This more or less mirrors the descriptive–normative distinction I mention above. More formally, for the purposes of this book I define the following terms:

the political class—national-level elected politicians;

the political-class narrative—a dissatisfaction at the perceived disconnect between politicians and the public that is seen to be a result of the lack of diversity among elected politicians in terms of one or more of the following: age, sex, ideological diversity, occupational experience, ethnicity, social class, wealth, morality, behaviour, desires, and other political views or attitudes.

At its heart, I see the political-class narrative as broadly encompassing the idea that members of the political class are increasingly like one another while decreasingly like the rest of the population. This supposed homogeneity covers their personal characteristics, their attitudes, and their behaviour. My approach has benefits when it comes to empirically investigating the issue of the political class. On my definition, we have a thing (national-level elected politicians) that we can study in order to ascertain whether some other things are true about it (its attitudes, behaviours, and characteristics). As such, we can study the validity of the normative dimension of the political-class question without getting this tangled up with the thing itself.

The Political-Class Narrative I: Personal Characteristics

The most common element of the political-class narrative focuses on the lack of characteristic diversity held by its members.[11] This might be the reasonably vaguely specified characteristic of working in a job that relates to politics before becoming an actual MP, or the more precise one of being a politician who was educated at Oxbridge,[12] for example. In either case, membership is contingent on holding these characteristics. For those who adopt such a narrative, the political class is simply the group of people who fit the classification of choice, or is a description based on these characteristics that is (sometimes erroneously) extended to all politicians in a chosen legislature.

Perhaps the most informative uses of the term focus on the ways in which elected politicians were engaged with the formal political system prior to their actual election. Broadly, this process can be referred to as one of professionalization, whereby politicians have undergone a process of training and assimilation into the political system not unlike those required in other professions such as architecture or accounting.[13] One of the key accusations in this part of the political-class narrative is that all, or at least a large number of, politicians are such professional politicians, with the accompanying insinuation that they have never had a 'proper job', and so on. There are multiple reasons that this process of professionalization has become something of a lightning conductor, the main one being that it fits with a broader narrative regarding the ways in which politicians are increasingly detached from the public at large. If politicians are meant to represent the people, the argument goes, how can they do this if they have very little idea of what exactly it is that the majority of said people spend most of their waking hours doing? On this reading, any professionalization comes to act as a sort of indoctrination process into the ways of the political class. This is not entirely inaccurate. The political scientist Heinrich Best and his colleagues note:

Both professionalisation and careerisation [sic] enable limited adaptation to change and a renewal of political personnel, since they lay down a path to office for new contenders and provide them with the necessary means to follow it. On the other hand, they establish rules and procedures that integrate outsiders into the world of insiders and keep out of the game those challengers who are unwilling or unable to conform.[14]

Occupation, as many researchers have previously noted, can be a useful proxy for social class, and working in politics for the majority of your career might be perceived as a solidly upper-middle-class occupation, even if the reality is probably far less glamorous than people may think. It is also a successful meme because it cohabits perfectly with another part of the political-class narrative, the idea of the 'Westminster bubble', something that is in turn part of a broader anti-metropolitan strand of feeling. I will return to how these notions of occupational and cultural similarity are often linked to misgivings about the attitudes of members of the political class, but I want to pause here and see if the data offers support for the idea, expressed neatly by Andy Burnham, that 'we're all professional politicians now'.[15]

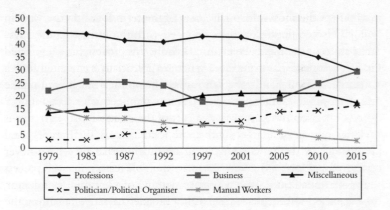

Figure 1.1 MPs' occupational background by election, 1979–2015 (percentage of all MPs). Data adapted from *The British General Election of...* series.[16] Data includes MPs from three main parties only, as well as the SNP in 2015. Politician/Political Organiser shown with broken line.

Figure 1.1 shows the occupational backgrounds of the majority of MPs returned at each general election since 1979.[17] I want to distinguish between the different kinds of pattern that we can see here—those that appear to be linked to whichever party won the election in question (either Conservative or Labour, or neither), and those that seem to persevere over time regardless of who was victorious. For example, when the Conservative Party win an election, the overall percentage of MPs with occupational backgrounds in business is higher. Conversely, when Labour win, the percentage of MPs with occupational backgrounds in the wider professions, encompassing teaching and civil service roles, is generally higher. There are two occupational categories that move steadily in one direction across the whole time series—manual workers, the number of whom has declined to almost zero in the past forty years, and political workers, who have tripled in number in the same period. These patterns have held regardless of who the election winners are, suggesting that they are not necessarily specific to any given party. In 1979, around 3 per cent of MPs had prior occupational experience in politics, either as a full-time politician at some other level of British government or as a political organizer.[18] The figure following the 2015 general election was 16.5 per cent. Over the same period, the percentage of former manual workers in Parliament has dropped from around 16 per cent to 3 per cent, roughly mirroring the change seen in the number of political workers. I am not suggesting that there was a direct switch between these categories on a one-in, one-out basis, as the patterns are more complex than that. What is clear, though, is that one kind of occupational experience has been essentially eliminated from national political life at the same time as another has been in the ascendancy. As I will discuss further in Chapter 2, this has had a deleterious effect on the number of MPs from traditionally working-class backgrounds in Parliament, with these former manual labourers not being replaced by individuals who have experience of working in these roles' modern-day equivalents.

An interesting question is why politicians who match this description have attracted so much attention. One possible reason is that although politicians who fit this profile are not necessarily numerically dominant, they do tend to be more prominent in our political life than others. In my own research I have found evidence that politicians who have worked in politics prior to their election to the Commons are more likely to reach the front benches than their colleagues lacking this sort of experience.[19] When you see a politician on the television news, or elsewhere in the media, he or she is more likely to be a frontbencher than a backbencher and is therefore, in real terms, more likely to fit this description of 'professional politician'. In other words, what we are seeing here is a kind of optical illusion making MPs with these kinds of backgrounds seem more numerous than they actually are. Again, though this almost certainly overstates their presence, it is worth being clear that they are increasing in number all the same.

Moving on from occupation, complaints about the political class have also focused on other kinds of demographic unrepresentativeness, most notably encompassing concerns regarding the low numbers of both women and individuals from ethnic minorities in political institutions. At the time of writing, women make up 29 per cent of the House of Commons, and MPs from black and minority ethnic (BME) backgrounds are roughly 6 per cent of the total. Although these numbers might sound low, they have improved dramatically since the 1980s, as shown in Figure 1.2.

As I will discuss in Chapter 4, these increases have primarily been the result of concerted efforts on the part of the Labour and Conservative Parties to increase their overall representativeness. Despite these improvements, the numbers of MPs in each group are low in comparison to equivalent numbers in the overall population, of which women

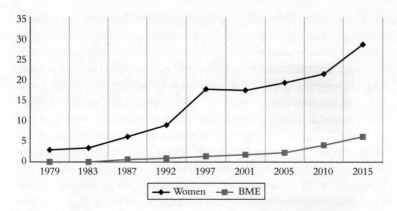

Figure 1.2 Women MPs and MPs from black and minority ethnic (BME) backgrounds, 1979–2015 (percentage of all MPs). Data from *House of Commons Library Factsheets.*[20]

make up around 52 per cent and individuals from BME backgrounds between 11 and 14 per cent according to various measures.[21]

In addition to concerns focused on sex and ethnicity, the political class has also been criticized for being significantly wealthier than the average member of the population.[22] This sort of critique was perhaps best espoused by Conservative MP Nadine Dorries, who described the then prime minister David Cameron and chancellor George Osborne as 'two posh boys who don't know the price of milk'.[23] It is, however, hard to accurately assess the question of relative wealth, due to a lack of reliable data. One alternative option is to compare the salary received by MPs to the national average, and on this measure MPs clearly earn quite a lot more money than the average Briton. However, this is not a particularly fruitful route to take—MPs, as a bare minimum, need to earn enough to make it economically viable and attractive to do the job, and if MPs earned nothing, sitting in Parliament would return to being the preserve of those who had independent sources of income. Indeed, when looking at older accounts of who our MPs are, it is common to find reference to the fact that they need a financial cushion of this kind.[24] This is not to say that wealth does not matter, as it does, but it is hard to put a figure on exactly how unrepresentative the political class is of the UK as a whole when it comes to money, at least while they are in office (in the section on behaviour, below, I discuss potential post-office gains). One possible proxy measure of wealth might be the percentage of MPs who are private landlords (renting out presumably second or other non-occupied properties), compared with the percentage of Britons overall. Figures from early 2016 suggest that close to a third of all MPs let property as landlords, compared with only 2 per cent of the British adult population as a whole.[25] Again, although this is just a proxy measure of wealth, it is indicative of a broad difference between the political class and the wider public on this point. The role of wealth in shaping the political class is perhaps more obvious in the United States, with some estimates putting the average wealth (or net worth) of a Member of Congress at over one million dollars.[26] To observers of US politics, this is probably not much of a surprise given the huge cost of embarking on a congressional campaign in the first place, something that is less of a concern in the UK in relative terms.

A further issue is that of education, especially the seeming dominance of a small number of elite, private, fee-paying schools and leading universities in enlightening our most prominent politicians. The available statistics offer support to those concerned about this, and demonstrate a fairly stark educational difference between the average MP and the average voter (whether this is a good thing or not is something I discuss later in the book). Looking at the composition of the House of Commons following the 2015 general election, the Sutton Trust found that 32 per cent of MPs were privately educated compared to only 7 per cent of the UK population as a whole. This was a slight drop from 35 per cent following the 2010 general election.[27] Eighty-nine per cent of MPs are university graduates, with 25 per cent of this group attending Oxbridge universities. Office for National Statistics figures from 2013 suggest that something in the region of 40 per cent of the adult population are degree-educated, so although the difference on this measure is less stark, it is still notable.[28] The Oxbridge influence on the upper echelons of the political class is seen as pernicious by some. Take Nick Cohen, for example, who writes in *The Spectator*:

If graduates from an architecture school designed buildings that were unfit for human habitation or doctors from a university's medical faculty left death in their wake, their teachers would worry. The graduates of Oxford's Politics, Philosophy and Economics course form the largest single component of the most despised generation of politicians since the Great Reform Act. Yet their old university does not show a twinge of concern.[29]

Why does education matter? Concern regarding private education in particular reflects broader worries about social mobility—or, more precisely, a lack thereof. Private education, in the majority of cases, is reflective of familial wealth, and thus of a more general set of early-life privileges. An amusing incident during a December 2015 episode of the BBC programme *Question Time* highlighted the prevalence of private education among the broader societal elite, which might include journalists as well as politicians. A discussion of the potential expansion of Heathrow Airport brought about the following exchange between Conservative MP Jacob Rees-Mogg and presenter David Dimbleby:[30]

REES-MOGG: I used to live not a million miles from Slough with the aeroplanes going over and I must confess they didn't prove too bother-some then.

DIMBLEBY [interrupting]: Eton, was that? [audience laughter and applause]

REES-MOGG: That's absolutely right...I was at school with your son.

[more laughter and applause]

Similar arguments, although less convincing ones, might be made about attendance at Oxbridge. The Sutton Trust, reflecting a commonly heard meritocratic refrain, argue that 'the best people should be able to become MPs, regardless of their social background'.[31] For them, existing patterns of exclusion are reflective of various path dependencies supported by financial and other social privilege.

Age is the final area of potential characteristic unrepresentativeness I will consider. The average age of all MPs following the 2015 general election was 50 years, which is exactly the same as it was following the 2010 election, but this is part of an overall downward shift in the age at which MPs first enter the Commons.[32] This is contrary to the overall ageing of the UK population; even including children, the median age of the UK population was 40 years according to 2014 data, the highest ever.[33] Age is in some ways trickier to discuss than the above. Often, this discussion is derailed with questions of maturity, experience, and intelligence. As with questions around lowering the voting age, critiques based on these things are generally misguided, and it is usually better to simply admit that age limits are, for the most part, fairly arbitrary (not that this makes them unnecessary). In order to be an MP, you need to be over the age of 18, and it is difficult to see that there would be any benefit from reducing this lower bound. However, this is also not the primary concern: the issue is that MPs are overwhelmingly middle-aged, and it has been argued that this results in a political sphere that is dominated by those who are also more likely to be securely employed and financially robust than younger people. This also seems to increasingly be the case given changes to patterns of employment and rising housing costs, among other indicators of cost of living. Traditionally, it might have been argued that this is not necessarily a bad thing, with it being only fair to limit political decision-making to those who have a stake in society. Of course, this interpretation relies on an assumption that only things like property and/or a family of one's own count as a stake, one that is now rightly considered untenable.

A more interesting point to consider is how the professionalization of politics has affected the average age of MPs. On the one hand, it feels that MPs are getting younger, especially those who appear most prominently in the media. On the other, younger people who do want to get into politics may increasingly feel that going down the professional route is their only option, tarnishing those who make it into the Commons with the impression that they are party drones from a professional politician factory, and so on. There are exceptions to this where a younger candidate wins unexpectedly, like Mhairi Black in 2015, but my own research suggests that MPs who enter Parliament having already worked in or around Westminster prior to their election are likely to do so at a younger age than MPs who have not. Looking at the 1997 general election cohort, the largest new intake since the Second World War, I wrote:

> The 1997 parliamentary intake is dominated by individuals of middling age, with nearly half of all MPs being elected whilst in their 40s. It is more interesting that 56% of those MPs with instrumental experience were elected whilst in their 30s compared with 24.8% of those MPs with local council experience, which, although not quite an invasion of youth, is a significant difference.[34]

So, although one kind of unrepresentativeness might be being dealt with, another simultaneously rears its head.

The Political-Class Narrative II: Attitudes

A second category of criticisms of the political class focuses on their attitudes, arguing that they all think the same things about whatever it is politicians think about.[35] Although this is a common theme, there is no agreement on the content of what it is politicians are actually meant to agree on. For example, some on the right have claimed that politicians are all politically correct, Europhiles, elitists, and so on.[36] From the left, the charge is that politicians are all beholden to neo-liberal economic ideas whether they realize it or not.[37]

There is little reliable evidence as to the content of politicians' attitudes. Primarily, this is because it is increasingly difficult for political scientists and other interested parties to survey them in any kind of reliably representative fashion. I also suspect it is because those who make claims regarding their content are not always as interested in backing them up with evidence as they are in making them in the first place.

I am not entirely unsympathetic to the notion that large numbers of the political class might share opinions on prominent political questions such as the nature of political infrastructure, the kind of economic system we should have, and broader questions about the views and capabilities of the public as a whole. For example, they almost all clearly believe in the importance of representative democratic institutions. They also all likely believe that voting is important, and I should think many lean towards the idea that it is a duty of conscientious citizens to participate in elections, especially citizens who have pledged to vote for them. A majority probably support the rule of law.[38] Once you begin to break it down, the claim that all politicians think the same way does not sound so outlandish, at least on a limited number and specific kind of subjects, although I equally imagine that a solid majority of the population as a whole supports most of the statements above as well. However, those who hold marginalized ideas about the organization of political life can accurately state, at least on the face of it, that their own attitudes are not represented in political life—most notably, those who do not feel particular affection for any of the political parties currently on offer.

Owen Jones's book *The Establishment* offers a useful discussion of how members of what he calls 'the Establishment' have unquestioningly supported the adoption of free-market ideas drawn from neo-liberal economics.[39] Jones writes:

The shared ideology of the Establishment [is] a set of ideas that helps it to rationalize and justify its position and behaviour. Often described as 'neo-liberalism', this ideology is based around a belief in so-called 'free markets': in transferring public assets to profit-driven businesses as far as possible; in a degree of opposition – if not hostility – to a formal role for the state in the economy; in support for reducing the tax burden on private interests; and in the driving back of any form of collective organization that might challenge the status quo.[40]

Although not discussing a political or ruling class directly, political economist Colin Hay puts forward a similar argument in his book *Why We Hate Politics*. Hay claims that politicians have almost wholesale accepted the idea that markets are more often than not the best way to make decisions that would have been seen as explicitly political in the past.[41] I do not want to dwell on this point too much here, as I discuss it further in Chapter 3, but the notion that a large percentage of the political class might share the same ideas about how best to structure the economy, and the size of the state, seems fairly central to this aspect of the political-class narrative.

A further part of the political-class narrative focuses on other attitudes, particularly a supposed political correctness, Europhilia, and a broadly metropolitan outlook. Closely linked is the idea that the political class is London-centric in its overall outlook. In particular, this line of criticism has been used by political actors of various stripes, most notably the UK Independence Party (UKIP), to locate themselves outside of this apparent Westminster bubble. In a typical case, the then leader of UKIP, Nigel Farage, defended party advertising campaigns that had attracted accusations of xenophobia as being 'a hard-hitting reflection of reality as it is experienced by millions of British people struggling to earn a living outside the Westminster bubble'.[42] Part of a wider effort by the party seeking to pit the European Union and Westminster elites against the rest of the country, the rhetoric of Farage and others does seem to align with academic evidence from Will Jennings and Gerry Stoker that the UK is home to a 'cosmopolitan-provincial backwater' division between urban and non-urban areas.[43] This has political implications, with cosmopolitan voters having more positive views of immigration, the EU, the state of the country in the present day (as opposed to thirty years ago), and gay rights than their compatriots living in what Jennings and Stoker refer to as provincial backwaters. Interestingly, however, both kinds of area show roughly equal levels of disdain for politicians and British democracy as a whole, suggesting that even if politicians' views might be perceived as being closer to those of cosmopolitan voters, this does not seem to have improved those people's view of them. There is no easy way out of this for politicians. As Jennings and Stoker write:

It is far from clear that national political elites and actors will be able to rise to the challenge of this new economic and political context. The public disdain for their actions from both sides of the geo-economic divide limits their scope for action. The new fracturing of politics is setting an agenda and a dynamic of political participation that creates intractable dilemmas for national leaders.[44]

The political scientist Matthew Goodwin notes the ways in which this geographic split played out during the 2016 referendum on UK membership of the EU:

Brexit owed less to the personal charisma of Boris Johnson, the failings of David Cameron, or the ambivalence of Jeremy Corbyn than to a much deeper sense of angst, alienation and resentment among more financially disadvantaged, less well-educated and older Britons who are often only one financial crisis away from disaster. They are the voters of old industrial strongholds, like the northern towns of Barnsley, Mansfield, Stoke and Doncaster, Welsh towns like Merthyr Tydfil that once fueled the industrial revolution, fading coastal towns like Blackpool, Great Yarmouth and Castle Point, and blue-collar but aspirational places like Basildon, Havering and Thurrock.[45]

Related to this, fondness for the EU has been closely associated with membership of the political class. For some, this is not surprising, with Peter Oborne arguing that of course the political class like the EU as it offers them another well-paid outlet for their insatiable political ambitions.[46] According to the BBC, by the day before the referendum an overwhelming number of those MPs who had declared their view on the matter supported remaining in the EU.[47] As we now know, the public ultimately had a different view, which might add support to the idea of a disconnect between the two groups on this issue (though, of course, these are declared preferences and there may have been various confounding effects here, such as social desirability bias; this would be supported by the findings of a survey of MPs in February 2016 that reported seven out of ten MPs expecting the public to vote for 'remain').[48] Indeed, it is possible to link the perception of Europhilia within the political class back to the accusation that they have swallowed neo-liberal economic ideas whole; as Peter Mair has noted, the EU is the neo-liberal institution par excellence.[49]

A final area where the political-class narrative has centred on attitudes is with regard to what members of the political class think about the public as a whole. Unsurprisingly, critics of the political class are harsh on this count: 'The Political Class is not merely separated from ordinary people and common modes of life: it is actively hostile,' writes

Peter Oborne in his entertaining polemic *The Triumph of the Political Class*.[50] On a theme to which I will return in Chapter 2, and one echoed by academic work on the subject, Oborne notes that, rather than owe 'their status to the position they occupied outside Westminster', members of today's political class have seen this shift, so that 'it is the position they occupy at Westminster that grants them their status in civil society'.[51] Oborne sees this as having a negative effect and discusses how 'the Political Class is distinguished from earlier governing elites by a lack of experience of and connection with other ways of life'.[52] In his view, this disconnect can be seen as having infected the ways in which politicians speak, campaign, and dress, as well as how they think the rest of the country behaves. Oborne is particularly animated by what he sees as the contempt of the political classes for the private sector and business community, as well as the disparaging way the political class assumes that the public consistently behave in an immoral and feral way.[53] He finds evidence for this in the way that employees in a standard business would not be able to get away with the kinds of things Cabinet ministers are caught doing while still managing to retain their positions.

Morally, therefore, and in terms of broader attitudes, the political-class narrative damns politicians for being at odds with the regnant feelings of the country at large. Often, this critique frames the issue as one of the political class being somewhat 'London-centric', particularly on issues of multiculturalism and immigration. In recent years, this has been fuelled by cases of politicians appearing to dismiss members of the public as 'racist' or 'bigoted', part of what journalist Brendan O'Neill has referred to as 'Project Sneer'.[54] Although I do not presume to comment on the accuracy of these dismissals, it is the very fact that a politician would undertake any such action in an apparently sneering way that has vexed commentators and been used as evidence that they do not understand the lives of 'ordinary people'. Zoe Williams notes in the *Guardian* that these critiques of the supposed metropolitan elite come from both the political left—'an explosion of rage at these urbane know-alls who love immigration because it makes plumbing cheaper, but never think about what it does to communities where plumbing used to be a really good job'—and the right—'a resentment of these moneyed cliques in which bohemianism has triumphed, and people who ought to be big and small "c" conservatives are now campaigning in favour of gay marriage and tolerating all kinds of previously insurmountable differences'.[55]

Some go further and accuse politicians of displaying outright contempt for 'the uneducated riff-raff who elect them'.[56] In the wake of the referendum on UK membership of the EU, columnist Tim Black struck a similar note, writing that 'the political class is now finally having to face up to its own reality as a ruling clique, infused with a paternalistic disdain for those it can no longer claim it represents'.[57] In a milder form, these kinds of accusations support the allegations that the political class makes certain negative assumptions about voters. These bear a great resemblance to long-standing elitist accounts of democracy, some of which I discuss and critique in Chapter 3.

The Political-Class Narrative III: Behaviour

In the same work quoted at the opening of this chapter, Michael Kenny writes:

An important strand of today's criticism maintains the sociological thesis that politicians, along with senior civil servants, figures from the media and occupants of positions in ancillary berths including think-tanks, political researchers and special advisers, now form an increasingly cohesive political class. This process, it has been suggested, has been propelled forward by the dissemination of the dark arts of political marketing and presentational techniques.[58]

A core theme here relates to the supposedly ambitious behaviour of politicians that shows them to be more interested in their own career progression than in either their constituents' interests or any ideology to which they have previously claimed to subscribe. In tow with this come accusations of careerism, which can most accurately be defined as the process by which individual politicians can make a sustained income out of politics by continuing to seek and win re-election over extended periods of time. This can all be linked back to the growth of political professionalism discussed above. The suspicion here is that if someone has set themselves the goal of holding powerful political office, they are likely to do anything necessary to make it there and, as such, they probably will not make for the kind of politician who the public claim to want—someone who will stand up for the nebulous category of 'what they believe in'. Speculatively, we could make the argument that this may lie behind the desire for seemingly more authentic figures which seems to run especially strong right now, with both Jeremy Corbyn and Donald Trump rising in prominence in 2015 and 2016.

Indeed, this suspicion of people who seem to be doing anything to get ahead in their political careers might also explain why the public favour those MPs who rebel against their party leadership more often, or who are willing to speak out against the official line. Research by Rosie Campbell and her colleagues suggests that rebelling against the party whip might act as what political scientists refer to as a 'valence signal' indicating 'integrity and trustworthiness'.[59] In contrast to career politicians who are thought to be willing to do anything to benefit their career, 'Constituents infer from dissent that a legislator is willing to risk punishment and personal standing within his or her party. Because integrity is a valence characteristic seemingly valued by all voters, voters see dissent per se as a positive signal about the character of the representative.'[60] To put it another way, voters like those MPs who appear to stand by what they believe in, even when they might be putting their political careers at risk in the process.

Another element of this part of the political-class narrative is the idea that MPs are in politics for themselves, seeking personal gain. On this view, 'British public life is once again dominated by a tight political elite which pursues its own sectional interest oblivious to the public good.'[61] Aditya Chakrabortty describes this group as an 'unholy cadre' and compares the kind of behaviour expected from current and aspirant members of the political class to that of cults.[62] Barbara Ellen, writing for the *Guardian*, highlights a case where leading politicians (or presumably those surrounding them) caused changes to be made to Remembrance Day procedures in order to allow party leaders to lay their wreaths at separate times. Distinguishing between 'politicians' and 'the people', she asks, 'Why can't they just look normal?'

I can't be alone in having been irritated by the unedifying spectacle of Westminster's leading lights seemingly grasping at the opportunity to demonstrate how wonderfully grave and statesman-like they can be. An anguished jaw-setting here; a wistful, faraway look there; an air of dramatised solemnity everywhere. Enough!'[63]

The assumption here is that the behaviour of politicians simply must be insincere in some way, in contrast to the way 'normal' people would behave in such a situation.

This theme of the political class not being 'normal' was revived when David Cameron ate a hot dog with a knife and fork. Matt Chorley, in the *Daily Mail*, links this to Cameron being 'apparently so proud to be posh he was happy to be pictured eating a hotdog with a knife and fork'. Presumably Cameron actually did so in order to avoid what Chorley describes as 'Ed Miliband's disastrous attempt to eat a bacon sandwich'.[64] Precisely how disastrous an attempt to eat a bacon sandwich can actually be remains unaddressed throughout the piece, but, of course, this may be worthy of further study in future. A non-food-related example came from Labour MP Helen Goodman, who inadvertently mixed up two villages in her constituency with the same name (Ingleton) when giving a speech in one of them. Leo McKinstry, writing in the *Express*, argues that 'Ms Goodman's error was revealing for it showed a spirit of complacency, even disdain' towards her constituency, but he also notes that 'there has always been a suspicion that she was just another professional political operator, parachuted into an area where she has no deep roots'. Comparing her with a previous MP for the constituency who had seen action in Italy and France during the First World War, McKinstry writes: 'That kind of experience is largely missing from the current breed of professional politicians, who have created nothing, risked nothing and know little beyond how to manoeuvre their way up their hierarchies.'[65] Although it is hardly common behaviour nowadays to have fought in the First World War, the implicit suggestion here is that many people create objects or businesses, take risks, and have interests beyond climbing career ladders and that this is not true for members of the political class.

Except for the expenses scandal of 2009, it has been difficult to provide evidence in a systematic way for claims regarding the selfishness of MPs, generally owing to the constraints of available data, but recent research suggests that MPs, either intentionally or otherwise, do seem to make some personal financial gains as a result of their time in office—but only after they have left it. Political scientists Andrew Eggers and Jens Hainmueller used data on the wealth of both victorious and second-placed candidates in close parliamentary elections between 1950 and 1970 to assess the impact of holding office on the finances of winners.[66] Their findings were mixed, with Conservative candidates who won and became MPs making clear gains when compared to Conservatives who came a close second, while Labour winners and losers had similar finances regardless of whether they held parliamentary office. Other evidence from Sandra González-Bailon and her colleagues focuses on the relationship between former MPs and civil servants and FTSE-listed companies in the UK.[67] They find that although there are a sizeable number of former MPs in non-executive-director roles, they are very much a minority of all MPs. They suggest that the effect might be localized to certain areas of government:

While just a very small fraction of former politicians and civil servants migrate to the corporate world after a career in public service, the majority built their careers in the same departments – an indication that such previous political and governmental experience and connections perform a significant role in defining their post-career trajectories in the corporate world. The evidence suggests that three premier departments – the Treasury, Foreign Office and Ministry of Defence – provide the greatest opportunities for access to the corporate world, with former public officials strongly represented (in relative terms) in the defence sector.[68]

A more sinister kind of complaint about the behaviour of the political class paints politicians as liars who wilfully mislead the public and do not come through on the promises they make to voters. Once in office, the story goes, members of the political class are no longer interested in keeping the promises they made to the voters when they needed their votes, but instead are content to pursue their own interests. This narrative has persisted despite evidence that it is not the case.[69]

Worse, assumptions such as this bleed into public perceptions of everything that politicians say in public, with this cynicism appearing to grow year on year. Prior to the 2016 referendum on British membership of the European Union, Max Hastings, discussing the state of both the leave and remain campaigns, wrote:

Public disgust is unsurprising when so few of the governing class trouble to pretend to give a straight answer to a straight question, whether on *Question Time* or in private conversation. A Tory grandee says, 'If they wanted to do anything so reckless, their special advisers would stop them. Every modern politician's spin machine exists to promote prevarication and opacity'.[70]

The notion of spin is intimately connected to the political–class narrative, as is the vaguely spectral presence of the 'spin doctor'. Peter Oborne writes that the term 'was imported by New Labour from the United States in the early 1990s, and well communicated the element of menace, subterfuge and mystique that had suddenly attached itself to the formerly drab and unpropitious post of public relations office'.[71] The archetypal spin doctor was Alastair Campbell, Tony Blair's press secretary, advisor, and confidant, who was fictionalized as the sweary and hyperactive Malcolm Tucker in the BBC political comedy *The Thick of It*.

A theme I will return to at various points throughout the book is that of how the media cover politics, and how certain kinds of media coverage might work to limit the range of individuals who consider putting themselves forward for political office. Critics of the political class claim that politicians are now obsessed with the presentation of politics at the expense of its actual substance. This is the core of what spin is. Kevin Moloney writes that 'to "spin" is to give the words describing a policy, personality or event a favourable gloss with the intention that the mass media will use them to the political advantage of the spinner and so gain public support'.[72] When one side of a political debate spins, so does the other in response, with the actual issue itself being relegated beneath the various claims and counterclaims being made.

Of course, not everything that politicians say is spin. Academics and people involved in politics who have written about the proliferation of spin are keen to ensure that not all political communication is tarnished with the same brush, and it is acknowledged that there is spin and that there are also political communications that are not spin.[73] However, owing to the growth in the number of MPs who come into parliament from occupations that probably have a lot to do with spin (special advisors to MPs, press officers for political parties, and so on), the perception of a link between political professionalization as a whole and the growth of spin culture among the political class will be hard to break. Indeed, these trends will likely be self-reinforcing. As political parties accept the logic that spin is a necessary part of contemporary political practice, they will professionalize its management. When some individuals occupying these positions move into elected politics, they too are likely to see it as necessary to political practice, and also probably favour those like themselves when the time comes to promote the cause of fresh prospective MPs. This is a theme I return to in Chapter 4.

A final area of contention regarding the behaviour of politicians relates to their conduct in the House of Commons. Anyone who has seen Prime Minister's Questions (PMQs) on television or in person will know that it can get quite raucous, with MPs on all sides shouting, waving, and braying throughout. Many, including the Speaker of the House John Bercow, have declared this behaviour to be undignified and even off-putting to members of the public who happen to see it. Evidence from the Hansard Society's annual Audit of Political Engagement supports his view, with data from 2016 finding that only

17 per cent of the public consider PMQs something that makes them proud of Parliament, and 50 per cent finding it too noisy and aggressive.[74] As I discuss further in Chapter 4, academic researchers have considered the possibility that this kind of behaviour in the House of Commons might literally silence certain kinds of MPs, most likely those who do not favour such overtly confrontational situations, and could well put off members of the public who feel the same way.[75] Of course, there is more to parliamentary practice than PMQs, and much of the daily grind in the institution takes place in quieter committee rooms, in relatively staid debates, and often behind the scenes altogether, hidden from public view. However, none of these activities are fully excusable within the political-class narrative. Even fairly friendly behind-the-scenes discussions can be seen as undemocratic, or reminiscent of shady cartel-like behaviour, if one wishes to paint them in such a light. For example, the development of the coalition government agreement in 2010 between the Conservatives and Liberal Democrats led to some claiming that the chosen policies could be 'seen by the public as a convenient excuse for undemocratic, back-room deals'.[76] This cry often arises despite the public also claiming that they want politicians to work together more often, compromise often being the primary watchword in such requests. On this narrative line, members of the political class are caught whichever way they turn.

Conclusion

This chapter has framed the discussion of the political class in preparation for the rest of the book. Distinguishing between the political class itself, and the political-class narrative that surrounds it, I have shown that the latter focuses on three main concerns: the characteristics of the political class, their attitudes, and their behaviour. This narrative focuses on the lack of diversity, in all senses, within the political class, and is to some extent supported by available data. The key components of the political-class narrative are summarized in table 1.1.

I have shown that there is evidence to substantiate at least some of the political-class narrative, especially those parts focusing on the characteristics and backgrounds of MPs. There is a distinct failure of representation to be found. However, I depart from much of what has been written about this in terms of what I think the implications of this are. Instead of

Table 1.1 Summary of elements of the political-class narrative discussed in this chapter.

Characteristics	Attitudes	Behaviour
Male-dominated	Ambitious	Self-serving
White	Metropolitan	Lying
'Posh'	London-centric	Spin-obsessed
Wealthy	Elitist	Badly behaved
Privately educated	Europhile	Using political
Professional politicians	Politically correct	connections for
Career politicians		personal gain
		Sleazy

seeking payback of some kind from the political class for these alleged crimes through personal attacks, or reducing their status by intentionally undermining their activities, I want to think about which parts of the unrepresentativeness suggested by the evidence might matter, why this is the case, and then consider how these kinds of issues might be avoided in future through the adoption of political arrangements designed with this issue in mind. This is perhaps a more, maybe overly, optimistic approach. Chapter 4 discusses what such arrangements might look like, but prior to that, Chapters 2 and 3 discuss why the evidence presented above may or may not be of concern.

2

The Case for the Defence

When teaching introductory research-design classes, one idea that all lecturers are keen to impart to students is the nature and complexity of the relationship between cause and effect. In an ideal world, we would consistently be able to clearly and precisely identify the causal relations between the outcome we are interested in and the thing we think made it happen. Despite seeming like a simple idea, it is often resistant to our best efforts in practice, especially when studying the social world, which cannot be manipulated in the same way as an experiment undertaken in a laboratory. Consider this example. An ice-cream manufacturer employs a new advertising team in April and they release their first new advertisements in May. In June and July the company's sales rocket, with month-on-month revenue increases in the hundreds of per cent. Delighted, the board of directors reward the new advertising team with a bonus, reflecting their satisfaction at the apparent success of the recent campaign. Were they right to do this? Did the new team earn or deserve their bonus? Unlikely. In this fictional example, the rather foolish board of directors failed to consider the possibility that the causal relationship between the new advertising team's efforts and the improved sales figures was not as clean and direct as they thought. In this case, the increase in sales was (obviously) down to the arrival of summer, and an increase in average daily temperature.[1] Behind the analogy, what we see here is that a fuller explanation of the phenomenon in question may lead us to consider the nature of the outcome in a different way to how we initially saw it.

This chapter does a similar thing to the emergence of the kind of political class I discussed in Chapter 1. In doing so, it offers a defence of the political class by way of explanation. Specifically, I seek to explain how the conditions for the emergence of the political class described in the previous chapter came about and, most importantly, that these were overwhelmingly not the result of self-serving decisions on the part of individual politicians. Instead, they are linked to wider changes in society, in particular the relationship between political parties and the wider public, as well as the relative decline of the political influence of the landed gentry in the UK. Crucially, though, this explanation should not be taken as indicative of my agreement with how these conditions have subsequently been exploited or how what they brought about has developed. For my counterarguments to the points made in this chapter, you will have to wait until Chapter 3; so, if you feel yourself wanting to scream out some of the more obvious rebuttals to the points put forward below, know that I will get there eventually. Regardless of any frustration it might cause, exploring the broader context around the political class, and considering both sides of the argument, brings into relief the issues at stake in a way that a one-sided polemic simply cannot.

Part of the defence I offer focuses on those elements of the current system that we should keep, another part on the likely motivations of our current politicians, a further part on a normative and instrumental defence of the status quo, and a longer part on the fact that various long-term shifts in our social and political environment have made the status quo somewhat inevitable to a greater or lesser extent. Finally, I outline the epistemic defence of the political class in the context of evidence suggesting that most democracies are in possession of a prima facie broadly ignorant electorate. In all, the chapter offers a potential absolution of the political class on two fronts. First, its members did not cause the current situation. Second, the current situation itself might be defensible on epistemic grounds.

The Defence from Access—Why we Have to Pay our Politicians

As outlined in the previous chapter, a core element of the political-class narrative focuses on political professionalization and careerism, specifically on those politicians who have worked in close proximity to national political life prior to becoming elected politicians. This has led to the establishment of a group of individuals who will often have made their living from politics for the entirety of their professional life.

Harking back to Max Weber, this is a group of people who live both for, and off, politics.[2] Some do not appreciate this development and preferred the alternative of preserving political office as a pure expression of civic duty that should be performed for no financial reward.

It is relatively simple to refute criticism of the political class that relates to paying them for their labour. First, it is clear that unless you pay politicians, the pool of individuals who can participate full-time in political activities without remuneration is going to be limited to those who have independent sources of income. As a result, you are instantly constraining the likely diversity of the legislature in question. Second, and perhaps more controversially, it is simply not the case that MPs are paid enormous amounts of money, and it seems more likely that they look to hold political office for non-financial reasons.[3] Compared to many other industries which attract equivalently qualified and experienced people, they are paid relatively poorly. Of course, they are still paid a significant amount more than the average salary in the United Kingdom, but looking dispassionately at the issue as one of simple comparison given the importance of the role, those MPs lucky enough to possess great fortunes did not establish them with their parliamentary salary. Overall, some may see paying politicians anything at all as corrupting them, but I argue that this perception is wrong. Regardless of any ill effects that may arise from paying politicians, paying them nothing is not a serious alternative if we simultaneously wish to have any chance of attracting prospective MPs from traditionally under-represented groups of society and of maintaining the impression that the job is one that society values.

Recent decades have also seen an explosion in the scale of the responsibilities faced by many politicians. Multiple developments, including the seemingly endless growth in email traffic, the informal obligation of MPs to engage with the public on social media, increases in the power of select committees on which many backbench MPs sit, and the significant growth in the importance of constituency service, have all increased the amount of time it takes to do even the basics of the job.[4] The outcome of this is an increasing difficulty, at least for many concerned, to combine this role with a further occupation outside politics.[5] In short, the scale of the task faced by most MPs means that we not only need to pay them for reasons of inclusiveness, but also because most will simply not have the time to seek out further employment if we do not. Additionally, the scale of the job means that MPs increasingly need to be willing to make sacrifices in terms of their free time, work–life balance, and public standing, something I discuss in Chapter 4. We are now talking about an ever-shrinking pool of potential politicians who would be willing to take this situation on. If politicians were not paid, this pool would eventually evaporate to nothing at all.

The Defence from Good Intentions—Why the Media Generally Get Politicians Wrong

Building on the above, a defence of the political class can be made that focuses on their public service and good intentions in the face of a hostile media. The argument can be made that putting oneself up for election, facing the public while asking for their votes, and subsequently holding public office, are acts of civic service that compare well with the negligible public service undertaken by the majority of the population.[6] This idea is reflected in the way in which we often discuss retiring politicians, thanking them for their service even if their own political leanings did not perfectly align with our own.[7] Some might argue that we should not lionize all of those individuals who hold public office regardless of what they do while holding it. Intuitively, this seems right, though democratic theorists and political scientists have traditionally been reluctant to be too prescriptive when opining on what doing a good job of holding office might look like. Suzanne Dovi, an American political theorist, offers a useful way of thinking about this question of how a 'good representative' might behave. For her, 'good democratic representatives are those political representatives whose advocacy work maintains and advances the legitimacy of democratic institutions'.[8] Specifically, this involves behaving in a fair-minded manner, building trust with constituents in their work, and aiming to make politics as inclusive as possible of those groups who were previously systematically excluded.[9] Neatly, Dovi's approach avoids us having to pass judgement on the substantive positions of politicians, but instead focuses on the way in which they carry out the role.

However, reading much modern media coverage of politicians, you would be forgiven for assuming that none lived up to these, or any other kind of, democratic ideals. The dominant narrative about the political class, as demonstrated in Chapter 1, is negative and assumes the worst of those who run for political office. This is not a victimless crime. As Matthew Flinders writes:

If the public truly 'hates' politics, as many scholars have argued, my impression is that this reflects the fact that the public's main source of political information flows from a media industry that peddles the lazy and cynical assumption that all politicians are liars, rogues, and cheats.[10]

Financial pressures on traditional 'old media' outlets have also arguably forced them to diversify the type of journalism they offer in an attempt to feed the insatiable appetite of a 24-hour news cycle that increasingly exists online. An example of this is the move to more 'process stories'. These, as their name would suggest, are stories about the process behind a political policy or outcome, not the substance of the outcome itself. Even if the term is unfamiliar, I imagine all readers will recognize this kind of story, where we hear about how a series of behind-the-scenes machinations, covert meetings, clashes of character, or drink-fuelled discussions led to a political decision being made, a decision often itself forgotten in the wake of speculation as to how it was reached. The Internet has almost certainly increased the volume of process stories, with Twitter, Facebook, and constantly updating live blogs becoming lynchpins of political coverage. I do not wish to make a judgement either way on whether these are inherently good or bad developments, but the cocktail of process stories and a never-ending outlet for them is probably not good news for those who are the subject of the coverage—members of the political class.[11] If the media has always been equivalent to a magnifying glass directed at politicians, it is now bigger and stronger than ever.[12]

It is hard to see how any one of us could survive this level of examination, or could think only good things of anyone who had undergone it. If we know everything about someone, it is unlikely that we will not find something we do not like. I might be uniquely squeamish about this, but I suspect not. I appreciate that some politicians arguably court attention through their social-media activities, and that journalists clearly provide a necessary service to the public overall, but focusing sustained attention on personalities puts greater pressure on the individuals who are meant to play along. This is an issue I return to in Chapter 4. If all of us had our work subjected to the treatment given to politicians by the media, it seems unlikely that universities, law firms, or schools would be as respected as they are.[13]

Process stories also tend to be framed as instances of individuals fighting over power—Brown and Blair, Clinton and Obama, Cameron and Clegg. Although the pursuit of power undoubtedly plays a key role in political life, these kinds of stories seem likely to frame that pursuit as being solely about selfish individual gain. I will give the final word here to former prime minister Tony Blair:

> We devote reams of space to debating why there is so much cynicism about politics and public life. In this, the politicians are obliged to go into self flagellation, admitting it is all our fault... believe it or not, most politicians come into public life with a desire to serve and by and large, try to do the right thing not the wrong thing. My view is that the real reason for the cynicism is precisely the way politics and the media today interact.[14]

The Defence from Party Change

One of the primary drivers of the persistence of a non-diverse political class, and its development as an increasingly professionalized class, is broader changes in the role, structure, and function of political parties in society. Peter Mair is one of the great scholars of political parties. Prior to his death in 2011, Mair wrote widely about the state of party politics across Europe as well as considering the broader implications of the kinds of issues under discussion in this book. He was deeply concerned by what he saw as a process of mutual withdrawal underway in political life—the withdrawal of the people from politics, and the withdrawal of political parties and political elites from the people. Writing in 2006, he noted:

> Previously, and probably through to at least the 1970s, conventional politics was seen to belong to the citizen, and something in which the citizen could, and often did, participate. Now, it has become part of an external world which people watch from outside: a world of political leaders, separate from that of the citizenry. It is the transformation of party democracy into 'audience democracy'.[15]

This withdrawal has had, according to Mair, the dual effect of citizens reducing their engagement with traditional political activities and organizations while, at the same time, these traditional political organizations, namely parties, have reduced their own engagement with the wider public. Crucially, this cannot be blamed on one side or the other—it is mutual, and ultimately mutually reinforcing.

How have political elites withdrawn? Part of the argument of this book is that they have withdrawn into themselves in terms of personnel. Members of the elected political class, as outlined in Chapter 1, are increasingly likely to have engaged in 'high-intensity' political activism prior to their election, at the same time as being unrepresentative of the wider population in other regards.[16] Mair discusses how this came to pass, highlighting how political parties were previously 'closed political communities...built on a foundation of closed social communities, in which large collectivities of citizens shared distinct social experiences...defined in terms of occupation, working and living conditions, [and] religious practices'.[17] Political parties took advantage of the existence of these cohesive social communities, mapping them closely to political identities rooted in 'mass parties'—political parties with large numbers of members. These parties would both represent the interests of the social group in the formal political process as well as hold office in their name if the opportunity arose. Mair writes that political parties 'guaranteed...representation, on the one hand, and hence government *by* the people; and procedural legitimacy, on the other hand, or government *for* the people'.[18] Many of us have a sense of what happened next, and how the era of the mass party came to an end, based on our own experiences. The rise of what political scientist Otto Kirchheimer called the 'catch-all' political party saw parties seek to appeal beyond their natural constituency (the social community in which their political community was rooted) in an attempt to win governmental office with greater regularity. As Mair notes, 'The desire to win office [won] priority over any sense of representational integrity'.[19] Over time, this has had the effect of uprooting what were once mass political parties from the social communities that held them in place. Uprooted and at liberty to wander, parties began to move with greater freedom around the ideological map. Aside from the electoral impact, this uprooting also changed the organizational structure and aims of the parties that went down this path.

Describing these changes, Mair asks us to imagine a continuum with society at one end and the machinery of the state at the other. As organizations, political parties will always lie somewhere between these two points, but over the past forty years they have shifted closer to the state end of the scale and away from society. This change has been concomitant with others that have affected long-standing societal bodies, including 'trade unions, churches, ... farming groups, business associations, and . . . social clubs', all of which were closely tied to political parties in the immediate post-war era.[20] For left-wing parties, those traditionally supported by workers, such organizations offered a path for private citizens from working-class backgrounds to enter political life and face the public at election time. As shown in Chapter 1, the number of former manual workers in the House of Commons has dwindled from a percentage in the teens in the late 1970s to almost none following the 2015 general election. This uprooting of parties on the left from their broader social base has certainly been a major contributor to this decline. On the Labour benches, many of these former manual workers have been replaced by archetypal professional politicians with occupational backgrounds in Westminster politics. This didn't happen only to Labour, but it has perhaps been a greater political issue for a party that historically had strong ties to traditionally working-class industries and the communities that existed around them. As Matthew Flinders notes, it was part of a broader decline in 'intermediate bodies' that 'traditionally played a role in cultivating political literacy and understanding'.[21]

Of course, the contemporary Labour Party maintains strong links with the trade union movement, but many of the kinds of jobs that replaced manual-labour industries as they were decimated in the final third of the twentieth century are either only very weakly unionized, or not unionized at all. Historically, it was not that unusual for men (and it was almost always men) from indisputably working-class backgrounds, measured by them having held manual labour occupations, to end up in the House of Commons. In perhaps the starkest example of this move from manual labour to the green benches, men like Labour's Dennis Skinner and Roy Mason, and Conservative MP Patrick McLoughlin all worked down the mines during their pre-parliamentary lives. Compared to now, class identification was once a relatively simple affair, with a reasonably clear delineation between working-, middle-, and upper-class roles in society. Since these MPs first entered the Commons, things have become more complicated. This complication has weakened many of the links between certain traditionally working-class occupations and political life as a whole. In their analysis of social class in modern Britain, Mike Savage and his colleagues who ran the Great British Class Survey find that class identities across the UK have fragmented in the wake of the kinds of shifts described above.[22]

This, combined with less rooted political parties, means we have not seen former miners, for example, replaced in the Commons by workers in the call centres that sit close to the now-derelict mines. This is not to say that the thirty to forty years following the Second World War constituted some kind of golden age of political representation—it absolutely did not, not least for women and ethnic minorities, who are now much better represented in the Commons. Parties back then were not particularly good at getting a diverse group of politicians into Parliament.

Crucially, despite success in some areas, evidence suggests that parties have not universally improved the representation of historically absent groups. Although there are more women and ethnic-minority MPs than before, there are now very few MPs who have held working-class occupations or who might be classified as being from what Savage and his colleagues call the 'precariat'—individuals at the bottom of the modern British social hierarchy, who have low income, low levels of savings, low cultural capital, and whose employment is often itself precarious or unstable.[23] We might say that parties have never been great at increasing the diversity of the political class, and although they have got better in some ways, they have got worse (or stagnated) in others. Importantly, the fragmentation of class identity found by Savage and many other class researchers suggests that building a political movement based on these social groupings will be increasingly difficult.[24] As Geoff Evans and James Tilley note, it isn't that class has gone away at all; rather, it is that the boundaries have shifted, with the working class becoming smaller in size relative to what they term the old and new middle classes.[25] In terms of explaining why the political class looks the way it does right now, these factors can bring us a long way; but more than this, they can also help us understand why the political class collectively doesn't appear to be an attractive prospect for voters to connect with. Echoing some of the sentiments of the part of political-class narrative that focused on their purported attitudes, Evans and Tilley write:

Increasingly, politicians are socially alien to working-class voters and, of course, vice versa: those politicians are likely to neither understand nor approve of many of the preferences of working-class voters. The modern left and its activists are particularly unreceptive to 'unfashionable' views criticising multiculturalism and mass immigration. It is not only former Labour prime ministers, per Gordon Brown's infamous aside, who view the working (wo)man as a bigot;

the professional left have never really wanted to believe that the group they champion can hold such 'unenlightened' positions.[26]

On the side of the public, further evidence of this disconnect can be found across almost all the modes of interaction that have historically connected parties and the public, namely levels of voter turnout and rates of party membership. There have been a number of comprehensive accounts of the decline seen in both of these areas, so I will keep my account here reasonably brief.[27] The authors who have written in this field make clear that, in terms of electoral turnout (measured by percentage of the electorate which casts a vote), there has been a decline across almost all of Western Europe. Some might argue that the overall shift is a small one. Reflecting on this, Mair writes:

> The normal expectation in comparative political research is that, while particular trends may well be noted in some countries, they are almost never universal. Some countries may shift together, but it is only very rarely that all, or even most, shift in the same way and at the same time. What we see now, however, is a much clearer indication of cross-national convergence in the trends that matter. In other words, not only are these now pointing in the same direction, they are also doing so almost everywhere. It is in this sense that the trends, though often small, are very significant.[28]

Turning to the case of Britain specifically, the drop is rather stark, with turnout dropping from 78 per cent in 1992 to 71 per cent in 1997, before the record low of 59 per cent was reached in 2001. The two subsequent elections of 2005 and 2010 saw a recovery of sorts, but only to a middling 65 per cent reached in 2010 and 66 per cent in 2015.

Compared to electoral turnout, party membership has seen an even steeper decline, though there has been a significant upturn in membership since 2015, most likely the result of the assorted kinds of political upheaval currently underway across the UK. Despite this inchoate resurgence, membership is still low in historical terms, and there is evidence to suggest that even though people might be joining parties in greater numbers now than they were in the previous two decades, their membership begins and ends with the authorizing of a monthly direct-debit payment to their party of choice. In short, this is not high-intensity political participation.[29]

Mair writes that across the period 1980–98 the UK saw a 50-per-cent decline in party membership; that is, 50 per cent of individuals who were members of political parties in 1980 had left by 1998. The only

European countries with greater losses are France and Italy, with 65 and 52 per cent respectively.[30] Based on this brief summary, it is uncontroversial to suggest that the electorate has at least entered into some process of disengaging itself from formal and traditional political outlets, with both the relatively cost-free act of voting in decline as well as the more taxing involvement of party membership.

There are a few ways to interpret these patterns in the context of the political-class issue. First, these changes in the nature and role of political parties can be seen as further evidence of a growing sense of disconnect between the public and the political class. In turn, this may have reduced the ability of political parties to act as a vehicle through which individuals who may not have been predisposed to holding political office could end up doing so. In other words, the location of parties, as Mair notes, has shifted away from the public towards the machinery of state. A second, alternative view is that these patterns simply underline the importance of maintaining an increasingly professionalized political class. If vast swathes of the public cannot be bothered to participate in formal political life, surely professional politicians are providing a service that society needs but that much of society has no interest in being involved in providing for itself. Perhaps instead of pouring scorn on those who take on the job, we should be thankful?

The Defence from Meritocracy

An alternative defence of the current political class originates in ideas of meritocracy, the notion that the best-merited individual for any position is the one who deserves to attain or hold it. This defence rests on the assumption that we can generate some description of what the job of being a politician entails. This is a controversial assumption given that even a cursory glance at the variety of ways different politicians approach the job right now, or throughout recent British history, will tell you that commonalities are few and far between. Some might even argue that making any kind of case that there are some definitive commonalities across approaches to the job is a conservative political move. That may well be the case. However, I think it is possible to generate at least some basic criteria, even if we might ultimately not find it to be a desirable path to take.[31]

Rainbow Murray offers a summary of existing attempts to do this, considering the criteria by which political parties and voters alike might assess prospective politicians.[32] Political parties, quite naturally, want candidates who share the beliefs of the party and agree with the policies the party wishes to pursue in government, should it win the opportunity. As such, they want people who have demonstrated their loyalty to the party in the past and who have given up their time or resources to help the party succeed at previous elections.[33] Related to this, parties will also want candidates who can articulate their message well in the print and broadcast media, who appear competent, whatever that may mean, who appear empathetic and able to connect with voters, and who seem smart. Voters often share these desires, though recent research suggests that they are also concerned with factors such as whether the candidate is from, or resident in, the area or district they are running in, the kind of jobs the candidate has had in the past, and whether they are relatable in a broader sense.[34]

This makes sense, for both sides. Consider a Premier League football club. When looking to bring young players into the first team for their debut, the manager of such a club will be looking for those players who have demonstrated their ability to do the required job in the best way possible. For many young players this process of learning will have entailed some kind of apprenticeship, nowadays most likely to occur in the youth academy of a major club or out on loan at a club that lies further down the footballing hierarchy. Similarly, accountancy firms seek to hire the best trainee accountants who will also have undertaken a lot of training, as do law firms, restaurant kitchens, and schools looking to hire teachers. In short, we have professionals in most areas of our lives—so why should politics be any different? If one accepts this line of reasoning (and I discuss why one might, and should not, in the next chapter), it stands to reason that political parties will look to select those individuals who have had the best training in how to be an MP. Where better to learn how to do the job of an MP than by actually working in close proximity to an MP before trying to become one? In terms of knowing the rules of the game, both formal and informal, knowing the physical layout of those buildings in which politics takes place and, not least, knowing those actors who *do* politics, individuals who work in or around politics in classic career politician roles can easily be considered the best merited for the job.

The Defence from Depoliticization

Related to this is a slightly more abstract, but plausible argument that sees the rise of the political class within political life as bound up within a broader tendency towards technocracy. A number of political scientists have noted a broad move, or desire for such a move, towards the depoliticization of core elements of traditionally political decision-making.[35] On this view, commonly associated with the 'third-way' politics that peaked in popularity during the 1990s, partisan leanings should be jettisoned in the pursuit of a politics focused on 'what works'. This can be seen as part of a broader consensus regarding the political goals that government should be seeking to achieve—namely, economic growth and, in recent times, a reduction in levels of public spending.[36]

In this vein Colin Hay talks about how depoliticization, the process by which issues previously considered to be appropriately subjected to political debate and malleable by human agency lose this classification, can take different forms. It can happen when political issues are demoted 'from the governmental to the public sphere'; it can take the form of 'demotion from the public to the private sphere'; or it can take place when an issue faces 'demotion from the private sphere to the realm of necessity'.[37] Hay notes that all of these kinds of depoliticization have the effect of displacing responsibility for decisions in the depoliticized area away from politicians and on to some other decision-making body, to individuals in society, or to fate itself.[38]

Thinking about the first kind of depoliticization—moving responsibility for decision-making on a given subject from the governmental to the public, non-governmental sphere—brings us to the idea of letting experts make decisions in certain areas. It might be argued that there are certain issues that advanced, if not all, societies face that have pretty clear solutions that can best be pursued by individuals with extensive experience in the administration of public services and other tools at the disposal of the state. In some cases, this is more convincing than others. The example of climate change is relevant here. This seems to be an issue that is fairly comprehensively settled in terms of the evidence base provided by the natural sciences, and the desirable remedies are at least partly clear. In such a case, do we not simply just want the best people for the job to get on with it? This might include experienced diplomats and other individuals with extensive international negotiating records. On an international scale, parallel to the national debate of single countries, would we not just want a few capable countries to take the lead and tell everyone else what to do to attempt to solve the issue of climate change? If this kind of depoliticization were to spread across multiple areas of government, the role of the political class becomes one of managing various expert bodies, not one of engaging in political debate, representing interests, and taking responsibility for the making of policy decisions. This logic can also be seen to have extended into the economic sphere, particularly in the period between 1990 and 2008. This is, of course, the logic of free markets: the more lightly regulated any economic sphere is, the argument goes, the more effective it will be. This logic was accepted wholesale, and still is to some extent, by the majority of political leaders in advanced democracies.[39] In this case, it is not experts running the show, but rather economic markets, seen to replace the 'perceived inefficiency of political governance to the allocative efficiency of the market'.[40] Again, the dominance of the market over political decision-making leaves the political class in a sort of caretaker role, watching over things on our behalf.

Another political scientist, Andrew Gamble, has written about the issue of what he calls 'endism'. This is the idea that we are seeing the 'end' of various core elements of society—the end of history, the end of authority, and so on. Crucially, some even claim that we are seeing the end of politics as we know it. Gamble writes that 'a persistent theme in western thought has been the dream of a world without politics and without conflict'.[41] This can be linked to Hay's third variant of depoliticization, which occurs when instead of being a subject of political deliberation and debate, something is transferred to the 'non-political' realm of 'necessity and fate'.[42] Politicians can claim, for example, that events beyond the control of any of us are dictating the course of policy decisions in any given area and, as such, there is simply no debate to be had on the issue. Former prime minister Tony Blair, speaking in 2016, invoked the process of globalization in such terms: 'My view about globalisation is that it's a force essentially driven by people, by technological change, by the way the world has opened up. You're not going to reverse that'.[43] In other words, there is no higher-level political choice to be made here—there is one way forward, and we must work within it.

How does this relate to the political-class debate? There are two obvious consequences. First, if the way forward is clear, there is no obvious benefit to be had in debating it, certainly not if that debate does not consist solely of discussion between equivalently qualified experts in that area. If no debate is required, the kinds of people present in the decision-making arena are of no consequence—given that they will not be representing different interests, or points of view, we could simply have 649 clones of one person notable for their organizational acumen (plus the original clonee), there to ratify the predetermined, evidence-driven decision.[44] Second, and related, if it is relatively obvious what the aims of political life at large actually are, this can act as a de facto criterion by which prospective applicants for those roles that deliver these aims can be measured. In short, and related to the previous point, those individuals who are signed up to these aims, or demonstrate aptitude in achieving them, are the ones who will be considered more eligible to hold positions of power within a political system aimed at delivering them. Again, the level or lack of diversity within the political class would be a non-issue.

The Defence from 'a Conversation with the Average Voter'

A close relation of the idea that political solutions are perhaps more obvious or clear than we had come to accept is the thought that, if this is the case, we should simply let the experts in these matters get on with the job.[45] This itself draws on a wider elitist tradition of criticizing democratic procedures on the basis that the average voter is relatively stupid or ignorant in comparison with political, economic, and other social experts. This case was pithily summarized by Winston Churchill when he said that 'the best argument against democracy is a five-minute conversation with the average voter'. There are two kinds of arguments made along these lines. The first is that voters are generally lacking in political knowledge and do not know much about either political systems or substantive political issues. The second is that voters are irrational and suffer from a series of systematic biases in their thinking that preclude them from making the best decisions they can. I will address these in turn.[46]

A substantial body of research in political science has found voters to be lacking in political knowledge. A somewhat unfortunate reality, findings of this sort are consistent across time and place. In the UK, for example, research has shown that voters are more than happy to offer opinions about non-existent pieces of legislation, do not know the demographic composition of the House of Commons, and have little idea of exactly how their taxes are spent by government.[47] Perhaps more troublingly, even those voters who report high levels of interest in politics seem happy to offer opinions on fictitious policies about which, given their non-existence, it would be difficult to know much for certain.[48] Many voters also appear to be fairly ignorant about wider social issues such as levels of immigration, the religious beliefs of their fellow citizens, the amount of money spent on social welfare, the number of people who turn out to vote, or levels of crime, to name just a few examples.[49] Given the importance of these issues in wider political discourse, and in the design and execution of public policy, it is not just a lack of specific institutional knowledge that might trouble democratic enthusiasts.

Scott Althaus shows, in his book *Collective Preferences in Democratic Politics*, that political knowledge is distributed unevenly across the population.[50] Perhaps unsurprisingly, he finds that 'knowledge of politics tends to be concentrated among those who are politically and socially advantaged'.[51] He distinguishes a group of well-informed citizens from those who are, on his terms, ill-informed. So we see that graduates, for example, are over-represented among the well-informed relative to their numbers in the overall population.[52] Demographically, Althaus finds that 'relative to the general population, the most knowledgeable citizens are disproportionately white, male, middle-aged, and married. The ranks of the well-informed also over-represent urban and suburban residents relative to their rural counterparts.'[53] These findings suggest that your social context has a significant effect on your levels of political knowledge and might actually limit the ability of social groups who generally have low levels of political knowledge to articulate their interests and political desires. As Althaus tells us,

This means that opinion givers who are ill-informed may be mistaken about their needs, wants, and values: they might give opinions that they wouldn't give if they were more knowledgeable about politics. Thus besides affecting the representation of voices, information asymmetries may also influence the representation of interests.[54]

In other words, individuals who participate in politics in spite of their low levels of knowledge might be harming themselves, as public policies that are detrimental to their overall well-being are implemented with their misguided and mistaken assent.[55] This assertion—that many voters might not know what is best for them or for the supposed common good—is supported by further evidence of voter irrationality offered by the American economist Bryan Caplan. Looking at how voters think about economic issues in particular, Caplan identifies a series of systematic biases among voters against markets, against increasing interaction with foreigners, favouring high levels of employment over equivalent levels of production, and a broader pessimistic bias whereby voters consistently assume that economic well-being is trending negatively.[56] Caplan describes democracy as a 'big common pool' where 'the social outcome depends on the pool's average content'.[57] For him, these kinds of systematic biases are a sort of 'mental pollution' of the big pool, and when the big pool gets to decide on economic issues and select economic policies, it therefore often chooses wrong. Caplan finds that better-educated voters are less likely to fall prey to the biases listed above, and thus are less likely to become pollutants themselves. In this way they are, according to Caplan, more like professionally trained economists. There is far more evidence along similar lines to that presented by Althaus and Caplan than I can explore here. Suffice it to say that the case against the average voter on the grounds of political knowledge seems fairly open and shut.

So, what is the upshot of this seemingly damning evidence? Caplan makes a number of suggestions, all aimed at reducing the political influence and impact of ill-informed voters. He discusses the possibility of giving 'extra votes to individuals or groups with greater economic literacy' and reducing or eliminating 'efforts to increase voter turnout'. By diluting the role that individuals who do not display higher levels of political or economic knowledge will play in the political process, he argues that the quality of the big pool can be increased. The pollutants will be left at home by virtue of not being encouraged to do otherwise. The political philosopher Jason Brennan goes further and suggests not only that the involvement of uninformed voters tends to have a negative impact on the quality of the policies produced by political systems they participate in, but that their act of involvement might be considered unethical.[58] He writes:

Voting changes the quality, scope, and kind of government. The way we vote can help or harm people. Electoral outcomes can be harmful or beneficial, just or unjust. They can exploit the minority for the benefit of the majority. They can do widespread harm with little benefit for anyone. So . . . I argue that we have moral obligations concerning how we should vote. Not just any vote is morally acceptable.[59]

Extrapolating from his argument about voters, we might assume that it can be more or less applicable in cases where under-informed individuals become involved in politics as either candidates or representatives (or perhaps even just as campaigners or participants in broader civic life). On Brennan's view, individuals do not have a duty of any kind to involve themselves in the political process. In fact, it is often morally preferable for them not to. In his more recent work, Brennan has argued that people have a right to good government and that a consequence of this is that individuals' rights to political participation need to be justified in this light.[60] That is, individuals need to show that they are in some sense capable of using their rights to political participation in a way that is not harmful to their fellow citizens.[61] In order to participate in an ethically consistent fashion, Brennan says, voters should be high in political knowledge and also high in rationality; in other words, they should know a lot about the area in which a political decision is being made, and they should make the decision in a defensibly rational way. Unless they can show this, they do not have the authority to be involved in the making of political decisions that will affect others. Brennan calls this the 'antiauthority tenet' and defines it as follows:

When some citizens are morally unreasonable, ignorant, or incompetent about politics, this justifies *not permitting* them to exercise political authority over others. It justifies either forbidding them from holding power or reducing the power they have in order to protect innocent people from their incompetence.[62]

Adopting the logic of this view, the kinds of people we might want to be involved in the political decision-making process will know what they are talking about; they will be able to think rationally, be in full possession of the relevant facts, understand the likely implications of their actions, and be able to weigh various competing concerns simultaneously. Additionally, we might specify that they would be well placed to implement policies quickly and efficiently, cutting down on bureaucratic waste and curtailing the suffering of those whom the proposed policy is designed to aid. Reflecting on this and what existing research has shown us about the political knowledge of the average voter, we may think the kind of person we may want to make political decisions on our behalf looks suspiciously like the archetypal professional politician described in the book so far, and who comprises an increasing proportion of the political class.

Professional politicians will know the key actors, processes, institutions, and rules of the game. They understand how things work. They are likely to be more effective at efficient policy design, at the process of legislating, and at navigating the vagaries of policy implementation than someone who lacks this experience and the knowledge it brings. Labour MP Luciana Berger, who arguably possesses the biography of a fairly typical professional politician, said the following after her election to the House of Commons in 2010:

The job that I did most recently in the three years running up to standing for Parliament, I was working in and around Westminster in both the House of Commons and the House of Lords and . . . I think it definitely helps to understand Parliament's processes, to understand the physical layout of the building . . . I think, because I had that experience, it's been incredibly helpful.[63]

In summary, if it is effective lawmakers we are looking for, we could probably do a lot better than to choose the average voter, and a lot worse than to choose a professional politician. Of course, this speaks only to the level of knowledge that these individuals have, not their rationality in making decisions.[64] However, a guarantee of one out of two is not bad, and is still almost certainly 50 per cent more than the average voter may be expected to have.

Conclusion

This chapter has offered a defence of the political class and attempted to explain away some of the more negative elements of the political-class narrative laid out in Chapter 1. The general idea has been quite straightforward: the development of a relatively uniform political class can be put down to changes in society at large. First, political parties have changed in both form and function, uprooting (or at least loosening) themselves from the communities of which they were once a crucial part. In turn, this links to our second change, namely a change in the economic structure of society, with clearly defined social classes that were closely tied to certain political parties giving way to a more amorphous and unclear set of social strata. Perhaps most importantly, these new social categories do not map cleanly on to equivalent partisan political divisions. Finally, both of these changes have taken place alongside an alleged change in the nature of politics. The age of ideological battle is over, we are told, replaced by a pragmatic politics of 'what works'. As such, bringing in a set of highly-trained, well-acclimated, professional politicians makes sense, given that they are there to pursue the goals that we all broadly agree are correct, not to debate their rightness or wrongness. Combined with a body of evidence indicating the general ignorance of most voters, when taken together these arguments offer a fairly robust defence of the status quo.

I have shown how the representative failure identified in Chapter 1 might be defensible. It is defensible on the grounds that even if the current political class *is* unrepresentative, it is epistemically superior to any hypothetical political class that would be more diverse and more representative of the population as a whole. In other words, this representative failure is actually a feature not a bug; one that selects for better politicians. However, the acceptance of such a line of argument requires the further acceptance of a number of not insubstantial assumptions. As you already know, I for one do not accept them. In the next chapter, I discuss why.

3

The Case for the Prosecution

Some things in life we do because we feel they have intrinsic value, not because we think that we will gain some other benefit from doing them. Other things we do solely because of what they bring us, and we say that these things are done for instrumental or extrinsic reasons. Arguments in favour of greater diversity in the composition of political institutions also fall into these two camps: some support diverse democratic assemblies entirely for intrinsic reasons (they are simply a good thing in themselves), while others seek to justify them instrumentally (they have better consequences or outcomes than the alternative).

In this chapter I make a case against the current political class, and in favour of greater diversity within it, considering both of these arguments in turn. First, I argue that diversity among political decision makers is intrinsically good in the sense that it best reflects underlying democratic notions of political equality. In other words, I make a strong case for a more diverse political class as part of an argument in favour of democracy for democracy's sake. Second, I consider the range of extrinsic, or instrumental, benefits that could be associated with a more diverse political class, paying particular attention to the idea that, contrary to the thesis set out in the previous chapter, there might be epistemic *benefits* to greater diversity, namely in terms of the quality of the decisions made by more diverse groups. Although my consideration of this idea ultimately falls short of a full endorsement, the possible existence of epistemic benefits unique to democracy is one that I hope readers will take seriously.

My aim is to make the reader comfortable with the intrinsic case for diversity in the political class, and also to demonstrate that extrinsic reasons are actually likely to be more compatible with this than we generally assume. Overall, those who support the idea of greater diversity among the political class should be reasonably confident deploying both kinds of argument. As I alluded to in the Introduction there is an element of discomfort when non-intrinsic justifications of democracy are introduced, the concern being that this could be a slippery slope—if epistemic concerns are that important, why not go all out and have a wise dictator rule? I feel, however, that we surely must already hold a view that combines both elements to a degree. If democracy had no epistemic benefits whatsoever, it would be unlikely to have done as well as it has over the past century. It should be the case that intrinsic arguments are foremost in any discussions of 'why democracy?', but if we are sneaking epistemic benefits in through the back door in any case, we might as well acknowledge this.

The Intrinsic Case against the Political Class

In this section I outline an argument against the political class that does not rely on any of its consequences as the source of persuasive power. At its simplest, the argument is that it is not fair for any one group of people to dominate the political apparatus of a state if that state claims to be a democratic one. How can we establish this? Let us start with the work of the political scientist Robert Dahl. He argues that there are two quite simple assumptions that, when made, result in an overwhelmingly powerful intrinsic case in favour of an inclusive democracy. He writes:

The first is the moral judgment that all human beings are of equal intrinsic worth, that no person is intrinsically superior in worth to another, and that the good or interests of each person must be given equal consideration. Let me call this the assumption of intrinsic equality.[1]

As Dahl notes, this is a difficult statement to argue with. The opposing view (that some human beings are of intrinsically greater worth than others and therefore their interests ought to be given special consideration beyond that of their inferiors) does not feel like a tenable position to hold, and is certainly not one that should be taken seriously in public discourse.[2] If we accept that all humans are intrinsically equal, it is then only a small jump to accepting that this equality should be reflected in the political sphere, namely in terms of having equal political rights in the process of governing a given political domain. Regarding this question of political equality, Dahl suggests:

If we restrict our focus to the government of a state, then it seems to me that the safest and most prudent assumption would run something like this: among adults, no persons are so definitely better qualified than others to govern that they should be entrusted with complete and final authority over the government of the state.[3]

The pertinent question at this point is, what constitutes 'enough' equality? Does this mean equal voting rights? Perhaps equal rights of assembly? More or less than these? As I briefly mentioned in the Introduction the standard I am concerned with in this book is that of who is actually present in the decision-making assembly. Framed slightly differently, the question would be something along the lines of, if some societal groups are disproportionately absent from the political class, and others the opposite, are people in the consistently absent group able to consider themselves the political equals of the latter? If one believes that they are, does this mean that equal voting rights, for example, are a sufficient guarantee of political equality?

It is something worth reflecting on. The political theorist Anne Phillips considers the issue in terms of ideas versus presence.[4] Briefly, the traditional view—what she terms the politics of ideas—sees equality as existing in conditions that allow citizens to exert some level of control over the behaviour of their representatives. On this view, aspiring representatives make promises to us regarding their likely behaviour and the kinds of policies they wish to pursue once in office, and it is on this basis alone that we should assess their performance and react accordingly. *Who* the representative is thus ends up being somewhat beside the point (be they a man or woman, black or white, gay or straight, rich or poor, and so on), as what we are interested in is whether they did what they said they would. If they did not, we can then hold them accountable in some way, most commonly at the ballot box. 'Difference', Phillips puts it, 'is regarded as primarily a matter of ideas, and representation is considered more or less adequate depending on how well it reflects voters' opinions or preferences or beliefs.'[5]

Over time, thinking about representation in this way ebbed, something that was at least partly a reflection of the entry of people other than white men into the political process in advanced democracies. Once women, ethnic minorities, and other groups historically excluded from participating in politics were finally allowed to, the notion that it simply didn't matter who carried out the business of political decision-making came under challenge.[6] Gradually, questions about the legitimacy and effectiveness of descriptively non-diverse assemblies have become commonplace, and I will discuss these later in the chapter.

For now, I want to remain with the intrinsic line of argument I began above, and discuss how this notion, framed in terms of political equality, can be extended to presence—who is physically there in the decision-making assembly. Primarily, this theme is taken up in the argument for political presence from justice. This justice argument is best articulated by Phillips, whose work is focused on the under-representation of women in political institutions. Establishing the argument, she writes:

> We can...ask by what 'natural' superiority of talent or experience men could claim a right to dominate assemblies? The burden of proof then shifts to the men, who would have to establish either some genetic distinction which makes them better at understanding problems and taking decisions, or some more socially derived advantage which enhances their political skills. Neither of these looks particularly persuasive; the first has never been successfully established, and the second is no justification if it depends on structures of discrimination. There is no argument from justice that can defend the current state of affairs; and in this more negative sense, there *is* an argument from justice for parity between women and men.[7]

The justice argument is so strong precisely because it is not reliant on any link between descriptive and substantive representation or any appeal to the broader consequences of, in Phillips's example, having more women in politics. The principles underlying the justice argument that she lays out can be extended to the present discussion. Instead of the numbers of women or men in political positions, we are interested instead in how a group with similar traits in terms not only of sex, but also ethnicity, occupational background, and educational qualifications come to dominate political life. Paraphrasing Phillips, what right would people who fit the mould of 'professional politician' have to dominate our political institutions? Of course, you could respond with many of the arguments I outlined in the previous chapter. You might say that individuals who fall into this category are simply better at politics. They know more about how politics works. Or you might take a different approach, saying that it is not their fault that they have been so successful in political life. Equally, you might question why we do not lay the blame at the feet of those who do *not* run for office. Are they not at least partly to blame for our homogeneous political class? In the rest of this chapter, and in the chapter that follows, I will argue that this blame game is pointless, self-defeating, and gets us nowhere. Instead, I make the case for thinking about this issue as one of political equality. Starting from the argument from justice, I want to outline the ways in which this particular inequality can be seen as the result of broader inequalities across society and should thus be rectified.

For now, consider the possibility that having the political class consistently dominated by any characteristic, or set of characteristics, sends a message about what it means to be involved in politics and creates de facto qualifications that are required before one can express political opinions.[8] It effectively shifts the goalposts of democratic participation, gifting a minority the legitimacy required to participate in full and leaving a majority without such licence. It is a question not of who is to blame, or of which politician has behaved worse than another, but instead is a question of who is considered eligible to participate in political life. And, more importantly, who is not.

The Case against the Political Class from Democratic Health

As established, the British people are currently not particularly enamoured with their elected politicians. Political trust is low, as is institutional trust, and electoral turnout has broadly declined in the last thirty to forty years. Although these phenomena are hard to link causally to any change in the composition of the political class, there is some evidence that the public are sensitive to shifts in the kinds of people elected to legislatures or to the behaviour of politicians.[9] On this basis it is possible to make an argument that links the two: that changing the composition of political legislatures might well improve our scores on these measures of democratic health.

Such thinking taps into the idea that there may be other benefits that come about as a result of an increased diversity of descriptive representation aside from those related to positive outcomes for members of that group in the form of preferential political outcomes in policy terms. Phillips writes, 'Descriptive representation matters because of what it symbolizes to us in terms of citizenship and inclusion—what it conveys to us about who does and does not count as a full member of society.'[10] This is often referred to as symbolic representation, though this kind of representation is less clearly dealt with, or addressed, in the academic literature, perhaps reflecting the complexity of analysing it in any meaningful way.

The thought here is that getting a wider range of people into political office will influence outcomes such as political or institutional trust. The political theorist Jane Mansbridge is the most notable exponent of such a view. She makes two main arguments in favour of pluralized descriptive representation that are not justified solely on the basis of changes they might bring about in the substantive representation of the newly represented social groups.[11] First, she argues that increased descriptive representation will help to create a social meaning of 'ability to rule' for groups who have been under-represented in the past and who may have had their ability to rule questioned. In most advanced Western democracies, this might include those groups of society who either have been historically excluded from acts of political participation such as voting or are still numerically under-represented in political institutions relative to their numbers in the wider population. Examples might be women, individuals from ethnic minorities, or people from lower socio-economic or class backgrounds. For these groups, seeing people like themselves occupying political institutions might catalyse a virtuous cycle whereby the initial entrants cause further members of the population group to follow in their footsteps as their self-perceptions of political efficacy increase.[12]

Mansbridge also argues that an increased diversity of descriptive representation will increase the de facto legitimacy of the legislature or political institution in question, particularly where there has been overt discrimination against the now-included groups by those institutions in the past. It is likely that seeing people like themselves playing some part in the decision-making processes in political institutions will lend decisions made by the institution an air of legitimacy that was previously missing.[13] In this sense, people are more likely to trust the intentions of the decision makers when they feel they have something in common with them, as well as respecting the decisions in some sense, regardless of their content. Although it would be plausible to make an argument that this kind of legitimacy matters in and of itself, an argument that focuses on the effects of this legitimacy is perhaps more compelling. As democratic theorists have noted, the ongoing stability and viability of the form of government under which inhabitants of advanced Western democracies live are dependent on the buy-in of the inhabitants themselves. In other words, things would begin to look problematic for democracy as a whole if citizens began to remove their buy-in from the system in substantial numbers.[14] Clearly, this is something we should care about.

So there are three aspects of this argument from democratic health: the issue of inclusiveness, the development of self-perceived 'ability to rule' among traditionally under-represented groups, and the question of political legitimacy. How do these relate to the political-class debate? I think all three are closely related, both to each other and to the broader issue at hand. Returning to the data I presented in Chapter 1, we know that the descriptive representation of some groups is consistently low in comparison with their numbers in the overall population. For example, the descriptive representation of women is low. The descriptive representation of individuals from black and ethnic minority backgrounds is low. Similarly, the descriptive representation of people who have worked in manual-labour occupations or in the service industry is low. For many millions of British people, it is the case that they can look at the House of Commons and see practically no one with whom they have much in common at all in terms of the lives they have led. We know that the current political class and the composition of our political institutions are not socially inclusive in terms of who is actually present in them.

The downstream effects of this have been empirically explored in only a sporadic fashion to date, but it does not take much imagination to build on what we do know to extrapolate further. If you are a plumber, a cook, work in Tesco, or are a secretary within a multinational company, you will look at Parliament, see who inhabits it, and on the basis of that evidence rationally conclude that the institution, and politics in a broader sense, are not for people like you. This is likely to create the inverse of the virtuous circle of Mansbridge's 'ability to rule' and do nothing to reverse the situation by which extremely low numbers of individuals among these groups actually run for formal political office.

The question of how this affects legitimacy is harder to pin down. Individuals do not see politicians as caring about people like them, but this is yet to translate into a wholesale resistance to the decisions they make. Isolated figures and incidents, however, can offer some insight into the impact this lack of legitimacy might have if it was ever adopted on a bigger scale. Russell Brand, the comedian and actor, gained enormous media coverage in 2014 and 2015 for his views on the possibility of a revolution in Britain. Brand's call for revolution entailed a complete rejection of the current political class, as well as the pursuit of an alternative to electoral democracy. He writes:

Cameron, Osborne, Boris, all of them lot, they went to the same schools and the same universities that have the same decor as the old buildings from which they now govern us. It's not that they're malevolent; it's just that they're irrelevant. Relics of an old notion, like Old Spice: it's fine that it exists but no one should actually use it.[15]

Invoking a typical characterization of the political class, Brand highlights how their distance from the population but proximity to one another renders them irrelevant to the lives of the former group. He goes on: 'One thing we don't want to do is replace one ruling class with another; we want power to be shared, not concentrated, and the role of the diminished state to be administrative and responsive.'[16]

The 2011 riots across England are another case in point that allow us to consider the dynamic between the political class and legitimacy. What happens when individuals explicitly break the implicit rules and norms that govern societal relations? The riots broke out in the wake of the death of the unarmed Mark Duggan in Tottenham, north London, who was shot by police officers. Rioting then spread across the capital and beyond, even as far afield as Manchester and Nottingham. In the wake of the riots, political commentator Mary Riddell compared the riots to the Arab Spring taking place around the same time, observing that the London riots were 'an assault not on a regime of tyranny but on the established order of a benign democracy', almost echoing Brand's ideas on the irrelevance of Westminster politics.[17] Aditya Chakrabortty, a *Guardian* columnist who grew up in some of the areas where rioting occurred, noted how it felt almost as if politicians were seeing areas such as these for the first time. He writes, 'Whenever telling other journalists or people in government about my childhood home, I might as well have been describing a tribal settlement in the hills of Orissa.'[18] This combination of elite distance and subsequent delegitimization of the established political process seems likely to be part of the complex causal process that resulted in this apparently sudden breakdown in the social order.

On any reading, the disregard for the British democratic process expressed in these two cases is stark. It highlights the perceived distance between a non-diverse political class and the population it rules over as well as the sense that few of the latter could break into the former even if they wanted to. I will return to this theme in the next chapter. We could, however, adopt the position of Peter Mair, as discussed in the previous chapter, and view this situation in reverse—that the distance of political elites from the wider population means that it is *they* who have disregard for the processes of British democracy, and so long as this continues unabated, we should probably expect to see further outbursts of resistance in this mould.

The Functionalist Case against the Political Class

If you want to learn to use a hammer, play football, or ride a bike, it isn't that much use to watch others hammer away, kick a ball, or cycle off into the distance—you need to do these things for yourself. This is the kind of reasoning behind what might be termed the functionalist case against the political class. If you want someone to run the economy, you might seek out someone who has managed large budgets in the past. If you want someone to run a health service, it might be worth asking someone who has been a nurse or doctor. In other words, you want the specialized expertise that is core to the functioning of various critical sectors of society to be there, and to be heard, when political decisions about those areas are being made.

The argument against the political class from a functionalist point of view is straightforward. By concentrating political power in the hands of individuals with similar types of occupational or other life experiences prior to their entering Parliament, we might be missing out on a whole range of other kinds of expertise that could assist in the better running of the country.[19] This argument was made by a number of academics throughout the twentieth century before receding from view for some time. Recently, however, it has had something of a revival in work from the United States that asks how the social class of Members of Congress, measured by the occupation they held prior to entering politics, affects their voting patterns on economic matters. Predictably, it makes a difference, and scholars have found some evidence of a link between the descriptive representation of 'working-class' people and their substantive representation across various domains of public policy.[20]

There is precedent for such ideas. Historically, thinkers like G. D. H. Cole and others in what was known as the 'guild socialist' tradition felt quite keenly that occupation was a sensible and desirable way to organize large-scale political representation. Cole and his contemporaries wanted to draw focus to occupational representation based on 'certain purposes common to groups of individuals'.[21] At the extreme, this could be taken to mean that certain industries would hold the ability and right to elect their own Members of Parliament. To the modern reader, this probably sounds somewhat peculiar. The notion that academics or bankers, or lawyers or teachers, could elect, as a group, Members of Parliament does not chime with the way we tend to think about the organization of political life. For one, it flies in the face of the general erosion of collective bargaining that we have witnessed in the last thirty to forty years.[22] It also does not sit well with the dominant normative idea that individuals should be empowered to make their own rational decisions about who to vote for based on their consumption of information from the political marketplace.[23] In short, one might object that people's identity should not be boiled down to their occupation.[24]

However, the very existence of these older writings makes it clear that this idea has not always been so alien. In particular, it underlines the fact that many have believed that occupational groups are deserving of specific representation and that this is something to do with the fact that these groups, and their members, can offer insight and skills unavailable from other parts of society.[25] A lot of the political-class narrative can be seen as growing out of this quite intuitive idea. Describing this idea of functional representation in 1982, Samuel Beer, in an argument that one could now imagine being used in a comment piece railing against professional politicians, writes:

As control [of government] extends into the complex and technical affairs of the economy, governments must win the cooperation of crucial sectors and show sensitivity to their values and purposes. Not least it must elicit their expert advice…in various periods of history the contribution of representatives has been thought of sometimes as primarily 'reason', at other times as 'will'. For the proponents of functional representation in modern times, this contribution is especially 'knowledge'.[26]

These kinds of arguments are not confined to the history books and they live on in contemporary political commentary. Writing in 2010, journalist Jonathan Isaby asked, 'Does it matter that only three of the

23 Cabinet ministers have been councillors?', when it transpired that the first Cabinet of the new coalition government suffered from a distinct lack of local-level political experience. A 2008 editorial in *The Daily Telegraph* asserted that 'few senior British politicians have had a life outside politics and they can hardly be said to have made a success of running the country in recent years'.[27] We can detect traces of Beer and Cole and others who agree with them in these words. The key point is that there are certain things that can only be known by those who have undergone the relevant experience themselves.[28] This knowledge can then be put to use in the service of governing the country and managing our political life.

There is another way to think about the functionalist argument that focuses instead on the conduct of politics, this taken to mean the way that political institutions work and the way that actors behave inside them. It is not uncommon to see arguments in favour of an increased diversity among the political class appeal to the idea that different people might 'do politics' in a way unthought of by our current set of politicians. We can refer to this as the argument from difference. A recent example that would seem to suggest that there might be some truth in this assertion is the way that Jeremy Corbyn, elected as leader of the Labour Party in 2015, has approached the weekly session of Prime Minister's Questions.[29] Instead of adopting what might be called the political point-scoring approach common to PMQs, Corbyn has generally taken a more subdued approach, sourcing questions from members of the public and avoiding pre-planned catchphrases or one-liners aimed at undermining the prime minister in a television-news-friendly, ten-second clip. A proponent of the argument from difference would likely put this down to Corbyn's background, namely the fact that he is seen as the antithesis of the modern professional politician.[30] Corbyn is invariably referred to as professorial, something that is presumably (sadly for academics) not meant to be taken as a compliment. Additionally, his seeming resistance to, and lack of interest in, any kind of media-savvy activity marks him out, and alienates him, from many of his (now former) front-bench colleagues. The argument from difference has also been used to look at the behaviour of women in Parliament compared with men. It is often said that women are more collegiate than men, for example. Women are seen as more likely to seek out bipartisan solutions, and they are more likely to express solidarity with other women by forming friendships on the basis of party and shared gendered experiences of the institution. There is even evidence that the nature and substance of contributions made by women MPs differ significantly from their male colleagues.[31] Similarly, we might expect scientists to debate policies, particularly those with some kind of relevance to their area of speciality, in a different way from a lawyer or banker. In short, advocates of the difference argument are fairly confident that different kinds of people will do politics in different ways.[32] The point here is that this might apply to politicians who don't fit the current political class mould; if we get more of those kinds of people into politics, change may swiftly follow.

The Case against the Political Class from Politics Itself

I have always entertained the thought that I would enjoy being an elite long-distance runner. Surprising as this may be to those readers who know me personally, it is a long-standing desire. Although clearly not that great a desire given that I have done almost nothing towards achieving this goal, my interest stems from the seeming minimalism of the entire endeavour. Out of all elite sports, running appears simplest of all—performance is judged on one metric, which is speed. If you are faster, you are better. To get better, you need to get faster. Unlike many other occupations where success is a contested notion, in running agreement on this can be reached without fuss. It is this clarity, this ability to easily identify talent, that set me on my flight of fancy. Instead, I have found myself studying the political world, and in this way as in many others, politics is not like running.

In the previous chapter I laid out a defence of the political class that hinged on accepting that if the solutions to the major social issues facing us today, such as climate change, were clear, we might accept the dominance of political life by a group of expert politicos on that basis. There are two main rebuttals of this argument. The first is that we simply haven't reached this point—we are not in a situation where we have no need for politics and likely never will be—and the second is that even if we were to find ourselves in such a situation, technocratic solutions are not desirable as they lack the legitimacy afforded by open political debate including a wide range of actors.

Recall the general idea that we might exclusively use expertise in various fields, particularly economics, to guide our political decision-making.

On this view, there is no intrinsic need for the clashing of big political ideas or endless debates about what is the right thing to do. We know the answer to that. The real question is how to go about it. Political scientists have referred to this notion as 'valence politics'.[33] The idea is that voters no longer decide who to vote for based primarily on the appeal of the ideas or ideologies of different political parties, but instead are inclined to vote for the most competent party. In other words, which party is going to be best at achieving the goals that have, we are told, already been decided on?

But ideas are still ideas, regardless of how much they claim not to be; endism, technocracy, or whatever you want to call it, still carries its own ideological burden. It is as much a doctrine as socialism, Conservatism, Liberalism, or any of the other classic schools of political thought that have shaped the societies we all live in. Andrew Gamble tells us that, '[A]lthough one of the central claims of some forms of endism is that the era of the great meta-narratives is over, endism itself belongs to these narratives and bears the impress of them'.[34] Voters may well be behaving as if taking part in a politics of valence, and the evidence suggests that they are, but this is on no account a politics free of politics, so to speak.[35] It is a politics rooted in old political ideas, and these ideas are still up for grabs, as are potential ones that may be yet to coherently form. All of these modes of endist thought are guilty of the same thing—assuming the existence of some concrete goal, or end, of politics: what Aristotle referred to as the *telos*, or as in my example of elite running, having a faster race time than my competitors.[36] In particular, Gamble has highlighted how all are guilty of seeing trends in the fundamental nature of the political world instead of the reality, which is cycles of thought that shift constantly over time. Of course, a trend better fits with the idea that your own political beliefs are advancing on, and beyond, the others. As far as you are concerned, the slow march towards (your idea of) progress continues unabated. Cycles suggest the opposite. They are telling you to enjoy your success while it lasts, because it certainly will not be permanent. Thinking that politics is over, or that the era of traditional political ideologies is complete, is the very worst of this trend-based thinking.

So, in many ways, politics is like flying blind: we might have a rough idea of what else is out there in the sky, but more often than not we will encounter unexpected surprises. The political philosopher Hélène Landemore claims that 'politics is arguably the domain of questions where we collectively deal with the unknown'.[37] If this is the case, and there does not seem to me to be any serious argument that it is not, at least in large part, the next question we face is how we respond to this fact. What is the best way to collectively tackle a wide range of questions that are mostly unknown to us ahead of time?[38] More precisely, *who* do we get to tackle them?

History offers multiple options, ranging from pure elitism in the form of rule by divinely crowned monarchy, or some variant of expert-driven government, through to direct democracy in ancient Athens, with modern representative democracy, as seen in many advanced Western countries, perhaps lying somewhere in between. These, and other approaches, can be characterized along a continuum from elitism to democracy. The accounts I offer of these different takes on the question are necessarily brief, but I will direct readers to further relevant material throughout.

The two extreme positions of this continuum are pure elitism and some variant of pure direct democracy, which respectively reflect systems of government involving the few and the many. Options involving the few have, over time, developed from monarchic systems to representative systems that instead invoke various notions of expertise or qualification in the selection of a political elite of some kind. Justifications for systems of this kind rely on the identification of relevant expertise, of 'knowers' who can be expected to perform well when the time comes for them to make political decisions. This is generally contrasted with systems where the many, not the few, are involved in political decision-making—systems of direct democracy, or in rarer cases a mix of the two, whereby a representative assembly is supplemented by a citizen assembly of some sort which is selected more or less at random, not elected.

As most readers will know from their own experience of the world, an elected assembly of people deemed to be the best for the job in some way is the most common political arrangement in advanced democracies, and epistemic considerations make up at least part of the justification for the dominance of this system. That is, the system is deemed preferable based on the apparently relevant expertise of the kinds of people elected to it and, in some sense, the chosen know better than everyone else. (The extreme variant of this argument was put forward in the previous chapter.) Taken to its extreme, this idea is somewhat disreputable and has a rather inauspicious history.

Hélène Landemore has discussed how this idea sometimes sees democracy as 'the rule of the dumb many', and the French philosopher Jacques Rancière identifies the motivation behind it simply as the 'hatred of democracy'.[39] These ideas underpin the epistemic defence of the political class, and have shown what is perhaps a surprising persistence within public discourse.

Despite this, I think these ideas stand on shaky ground. Indeed, if we expect most people to accept the two basic tenets underlying the notion of political equality that I laid out at the start of the chapter, the only scraps with which we are left to clothe any defence of exclusivity when choosing our political decision-makers are those relating to competence or knowledge.[40] Along these lines, there is a general aversion to the idea that our politicians will be making their first appearance on the national political stage when they first tread the boards; rather, we expect them to have been in fairly lengthy rehearsals first. Consequently, we may have a broad preference for someone with a great deal more political experience than the average person in the street.

However, in recent years the notion that the 'dumb many' are that dumb at all has been brought into question by a mix of empirical and theoretical evidence. First, there have been a number of initiatives in recent years that have allowed regular citizens, often chosen at random (or as close to random as possible), to participate in citizen assemblies and conventions designed to gather the input of 'normal people' on complicated political issues. Examples from Australia, Canada, Ireland, and the UK, to name but a few, have all demonstrated the ability of citizens not intensely engaged in the political process to learn about complex issue areas, deliberate about them together, and subsequently generate policy proposals.[41] Empirically, the argument that the kinds of decisions that politicians need to make can only be made by those with 'political expertise' seems weak. On reflection, this is not surprising given the fact that it is not abundantly clear what kind of knowledge, at the individual level, would be either necessary or sufficient to tackle the range of problems faced by politicians.

Take, for example, the measures of political intelligence or knowledge most commonly used in political science, and other social sciences such as sociology and psychology. Traditionally, these will ask respondents a battery of questions, such as 'How many MPs serve on a select committee?' or 'What share of the national welfare budget is spent on unemployment benefit?' At the time of writing, the 'political knowledge' section of the most recent round of the British Election Study (in 2015) asked respondents to assess as either true or false whether polling stations close at 10 p.m. on election day, whether only taxpayers could vote, and whether MPs from different parties sat on parliamentary committees, among other questions.[42] These kinds of questions are really useful to social scientists looking to explain patterns of political behaviour or attitudes, but it is less clear that someone who scored highly on these kinds of questions would actually be a better political decision maker, and thus a better politician, than someone who did not.[43] As Hélène Landemore writes, 'The difficulty of establishing a causal link between low information level and political competence comes also from the lack of a good empirical benchmark for political competence that would be distinct from a good benchmark for information level.'[44] Despite this, the proliferation of professional politicians suggests that political parties, in a roundabout way, do think this, or it at least suggests that they wish to reward perceived competence for the kinds of reasons mentioned earlier.

Returning to the ideas of Jason Brennan discussed in the previous chapter, we can also see how using such a measure of political knowledge to assess whether an individual is fit to hold political authority as either a voter or office holder is problematic.[45] Good performance on these sorts of tasks is consistently correlated with particular demographic traits. As Brennan acknowledges,

If the United States were to start using a voter qualification exam right now, such as an exam that *I* got to design, I'd expect that the people who pass the exam would be disproportionately white, upper-middle- to upper-class, educated, employed males. The problem here isn't that I'm racist, sexist, or classist…Instead, the problem would be that there are underlying injustices that tend to make it so that some groups are more likely to be knowledgeable than others. My view is rather than insist everyone vote, we should *fix* those underlying injustices. Let's treat the disease, not the symptoms.[46]

On the face of it, this sounds quite reasonable. Brennan draws on empirical studies that show how high-knowledge voters hold distinct policy preferences to low-knowledge voters, and he argues that the preferences of this group will be better at dealing with the kinds of systemic injustices that cause political inequalities in the first instance. Again, this has an intuitive appeal: if there are a group of people who know how to best rectify social inequality, why are we not simply letting them get on with this job? However, once we pause for thought, it is clear that this is not so much offering a solution to the problem, but rather running away from it, arms flailing. One obvious refutation of Brennan's case for epistocracy is that, to a greater or lesser extent, we already have one. As I discussed in Chapter 1, nearly all MPs are degree-educated and would presumably perform extremely well in Brennan's knowledge exam. Alongside this, almost half of the adult population have a degree, and we know that degree-educated people are more likely to vote than those who did not attend university. Despite the apparently high levels of education among existing office holders and those who are more involved in politics generally, we are yet to witness the emergence of Brennan's egalitarian panacea. I suspect, based on his statements about the nature of politics, that this is because our current politicians disagree on the correct response to inequality based on various forms of ignorance and lack of knowledge, even if they agree that it is a problem that needs to be solved.[47] But it is not clear that Brennan's remedy would change this. As anyone who knows academics, or other professional and highly educated people, will testify, finding agreement among them is not easy. And in such a case, where disagreement over what is good, or what is the right answer, arises, truly political questions come to the fore once more. At the end of it, not everyone does agree that egalitarianism is a goal worth pursuing.

The point here is not to say that knowledge is useless in political debate, something clearly not the case, but instead to highlight that suggesting we can always know a priori what kinds of knowledge are going to be the most useful in any given case is misguided, and that treating this kind of political trivia as a qualification to participate effectively in political decision-making is wrong-headed. Again, Landemore summarizes that 'in a democratic view, there is genuine agnosticism as to who knows best and what the right answer is, at least at the outset. Who knows best and the what the right answers are can be determined only on the merits of different claims competing in public space.'[48] She distinguishes between 'factual' and 'value' questions in politics. Facts are fairly self-explanatory, and would probably be reflective of the batteries of political-knowledge questions I described above. Arguably, however, when facts collide with the arena of political debate, it becomes far less obvious where the line between factual questions and value questions can be drawn. For example, there is the initial question of whether a fact is relevant to a debate, then the question of the provenance of a given fact, not to mention the further question of how a fact should be interpreted. This is before we acknowledge that the majority of political questions are not simply factual in nature, but also involve values. For example, although two sides debating the benefits or otherwise of immigration to a country might eventually agree on a set of facts (the number of immigrants, the effects of immigration on wages or housing, and so on), there does not exist a specific number, or fact, that automatically makes either side 'right' or 'wrong' in the absence of some value set which is brought to bear on the debate.

The Instrumental Case against the Political Class

Above, I discussed how some of the assumptions underpinning the idea that expert, or limited, rule is better than inclusive rule might be wrong. Essentially, I claimed that the foundations of the argument can be seen as unsound in multiple ways. This section is different, turning instead to consider the possibility that, in addition to the assumptions behind the view being wrong, those who posit it are additionally incorrect about its likely effects. Here, I consider ongoing research from multiple academic disciplines that offers evidence to the effect that inclusive decision-making results in better outcomes than its exclusive counterpart. In other words, along with being just and intrinsically good, diversity may have instrumental or extrinsic value.

Driving much of this thought is the influential work of social scientists Lu Hong and Scott Page. Together, they have developed a mathematical model of decision-making that suggests that when solving a wide range of problems (like the political problems discussed above) or making predictions about the outcome of adopting different policies, for example, the soundest strategy is not to pick the smartest or 'best' problem-solvers from the population, but instead to pick as diverse a group of problem-solvers as possible. They write:

When selecting a problem-solving team from a diverse population of intelligent agents, a team of randomly selected agents outperforms a team comprised of the best-performing agents. This result relies on the intuition that, as the initial pool of problem solvers becomes large, the best-performing agents necessarily become similar in the space of problem solvers. Their relatively greater ability is more than offset by their lack of problem-solving diversity.[49]

To restate their point, the 'best-performing agents' (i.e. the brightest and the best) are going to be more alike overall, which hinders their collective problem-solving ability. If true, this is unfortunate given that this approach is broadly the one that has been adopted when selecting members of legislatures around the world.

How could this be the case? Surely it makes more sense to select the brightest and the best people that we can to make political decisions? Hong and Page identify how each of us approaches a given problem with both an 'internal representation' of it, which they refer to as a 'perspective', and 'algorithms...use[d] to locate solutions', which they term 'heuristics'. 'Together,' they write, 'a perspective-heuristic pair creates a mapping from the space of possible solutions to itself. A diverse group is one whose agents' mappings are diverse.'[50] Page also describes how individuals bring diverse interpretations ('ways of categorizing') and diverse predictive models ('ways of inferring cause and effect') to problem-solving situations.[51] In simple terms, this can be taken to mean that different kinds of people bring different things to the table when seeking a solution to a problem. Specifically, not only will different kinds of people *see* the problem in different ways, they will have different *tools* that they generally use to solve problems, different ways of *categorizing* the nature of the problem, and different notions of how certain actions might stand in *causal relation* to others.[52] Diversity along all of these lines can be collectively referred to as cognitive diversity.

There are four main ideas underpinning the work of Hong and Page, two applying to cases of problem-solving and two others to cases of prediction. For problem-solving, the first idea is that *diversity trumps homogeneity*: '[a] collection of people with diverse perspectives and heuristics outperform collections of people who rely on homogeneous perspectives and heuristics'. Second, *diversity trumps ability*: 'random collections of intelligent problem solvers can outperform collections of the best individual problem solvers'.[53] In cases of prediction, where decision makers have to choose between options before them, their first result is the *Diversity Prediction Theorem*, showing that the accuracy of predictions is just as dependent on cognitive diversity among the predictors as it is on their individual ability. Second is the *Crowds Beat Averages Law*, which shows that 'the group necessarily predicts more accurately than its average member'.[54]

I will generally focus here on cases of problem-solving, not of prediction, as it strikes me that politics is perhaps closer as an endeavour to the former. If you want more information on the mechanics of their theories on predictive cases, I have included these in the endnotes. Landemore, seeking to apply the insights of Hong and Page's work to thinking about the workings of democracy, argues that the mechanism that drives the above results in cases of problem-solving is deliberation between problem-solving agents, while their results on prediction (discussed below) rely on patterns of majority rule. Her overall argument is that cognitive diversity should be maximized to also maximize the subsequent benefits of this diversity during a process of deliberation. But what exactly is deliberation?

At its simplest, deliberation can be seen as an exchange of arguments by deliberators who seek to put forward what they see as the best argument in favour of their position, hoping to convince their interlocutor.[55] Deliberation, in theory, offers multiple benefits. It gives participants the chance to refine their own views; it may bring new ideas to the table; it can help us discriminate between good and bad ideas; and it can help us reach some agreement on the most desirable outcome.[56]

Many of those who have written about deliberative democracy see an outcome of consensus or agreement as its primary aim and see this as constitutive of what deliberation itself is about in a deeper sense. Among this group, there is a desire for agreement between the deliberators come the end of it, and a desire that the outcome of the deliberation should be justifiable in a rational way.[57] As Landemore summarizes this stricter version of the concept, 'Deliberators are expected, in the ideal speech situation where there are no time and information constraints, to reach an uncoerced agreement on the "better argument"'.[58] Others, though, are less strict about outcomes and allow for other kinds of decisions to be deemed legitimate. These include decisions made whereby people might not agree, but instead do not oppose a certain outcome, or what Landemore and Page have termed 'positive dissensus', which is a kind of deliberative disagreement but one in which the deliberators have refined their reasons for holding the positions that they do through the deliberative process.[59] The heart of the theoretical disagreement in this literature is whether deliberation has, by definition, failed if a vote (or some other kind of measure to stop the deliberation) is required and consensus isn't achieved. My view is that in most cases the distinction between deliberation and majority rule is not fine-grained, if indeed it is a plausible distinction to make at all.

For example, majority rule can often act as something that calls deliberation to a halt, or alternatively where deliberation is ongoing throughout a series of majority-rule decisions. Take the example of a piece of legislation passing through Parliament. There are multiple occasions for legislators to deliberate with one another, to discuss these deliberations with constituents, friends, and family, to revise their views or harden their original position, and to vote differently on each of these occasions as a result. Surely, the more important issue here is ensuring that the deliberation itself is meaningful and genuine.

Naturally, how to do this is also contested, but there seems to be agreement that deliberation can only earn its title when participants make a genuine effort to engage with the arguments of their interlocutor, consider the pros and cons of their propositions in a serious way, and make a reasonable assessment about their accuracy or validity. This is not just a chat or discussion where two people talk past each other, both merely stating their views. Debate is required, as is reasoned consideration of each position. This kind of high-quality deliberation can be encouraged through institutional design. For example, political scientists have discussed how the layout of the room or chamber in which a legislative debate is taking place might affect the tone employed by participants. In addition to this, the way in which the political culture rewards or punishes participants' behaviour will matter. Consider again Prime Minister's Questions. At a time when journalists are falling over each other in their attempts to offer a 'final score' on which politician 'won' the session of questioning while the prime minister is still retaking her seat, it is obvious that deliberation of the kind described above is not being encouraged. Admittedly, you might think that this is not the point of PMQs, and that holding the prime minister to account and behaving in such a way that will increase your chances of 'winning' are not incompatible, something that is likely true to an extent. Regardless, the research I discuss in this chapter suggests that this approach will reduce the overall epistemic benefits afforded by the process, and that a more deliberative approach would increase them. Available empirical evidence offers support for this idea.[60]

Still, there is a spanner in the works here. Page notes that 'diverse fundamental preferences frustrate the process of making choices'.[61] He states that these results hold only when the decision-makers have in mind a single goal, referred to as their fundamental preference. So, for example, the fundamental goal might be to travel from point A to point B, or to construct a new library. However, the theorems allow divergence in *instrumental preferences*, which are subordinate to fundamental preferences but are more often than not the actual point of disagreement between decision makers. Returning to the examples I just gave, decision makers might disagree on whether the train or the bus was the quickest way to get from point A to point B, or they might disagree on which architectural style would be best suited to the purpose of the new library they are constructing. In both cases, there is disagreement at the level of the instrumental preferences of agents, but not at the fundamental level: they all still want to get from A to B, and they all still want to construct the library. The question relevant to our purposes is whether we can assume that, when making political decisions, legislators in representative assemblies meet these criteria—do they share a fundamental preference even if they diverge in terms of instrumental preferences?

As I will discuss further in a moment, it is hard to think that they do share fundamental preferences in many instances. Although we might be able to find this in certain debates around technicalities in given policies, it is unlikely that attitudes even on seemingly minor points such as this are not in some way reflective of deeper political attitudes, attitudes that ultimately stem from fundamental disagreements about the nature of society—that is, explicitly *political* disagreements.

Why We Might Resist an Instrumental Argument

Although much of the evidence in favour of the epistemic benefits of inclusive decision-making is convincing on the face of it, there are a number of potential objections that preclude a full-throated endorsement of the idea. These mostly take issue with the assumptions required about the various moving parts described above for the full force of the instrumental epistemic argument to ring true.

The main problem is with the characterization of politics needed for the strongest form of the instrumental argument to hold. For it to work, politics needs to be a domain in which we are able to judge outcomes against some standard that is unrelated to the procedure that generated them. In other words, we need to be able to say whether political outcomes themselves are good or bad, better or worse, without reference to how the decisions that caused them were made. Landemore's

view is that 'rightness' might be defined 'in part in relation to a shared
set of public values that cannot claim universal but merely local validity
(e.g., a certain view of the hierarchy between equality and freedom)
but in part, also, with a smaller core of values that have universal validity
(e.g., the ideal of human rights and a number of basic freedoms)'.[62]
This 'hybrid' approach feels quite close to our intuitions about these
kinds of issues, allowing for certain kinds of outcomes to always be
right or wrong, and for others to be conditionally right or wrong, or
better or worse. Despite this, invoking a greater likelihood of 'rightness'
as part of a justification for democratic diversity still feels somewhat
uncomfortable. Although Landemore's position feels intuitively right,
it is hard to say much about it that is more specific than that. If pushed
to formalize any kind of standard on this front, one is inevitably smug-
gling various unspoken assumptions into the mix. Put simply, it really
is not clear that any such independent standard could be constructed,
thanks to the fact that politics goes all the way down.

This is because the idea that we could ever theorize a procedure-
independent standard of goodness or rightness is nested within a
bigger assumption about what politics both is in terms of how political
questions arise in the first place and, once we are in a political context,
what politics is actually for. Developing the analogy of flying I used
earlier in the chapter, politics is not just flying blind, it is flying blind
without a predetermined destination and without agreement that
flying is even the best method with which we should navigate the
skies. The utility of politics, and a necessary condition for its existence,
is disagreement on this very point.

It can be argued that politics is not really about problem-solving at
all, at least for the most part, but is instead about problem identification and problem framing. As Russell Muirhead beautifully puts it,
'Democratic politics is not just a tool to "get it right"; it is a contest
over what it means to get it right'.[63] This objection is quite simple: for
most of the most passionately debated areas of politics, it is not the
relative effectiveness of different solutions that is being fought over; it
is either a) whether this issue is even a problem that needs to be
addressed, or b) what a successful handling of it would look like. This
becomes clear when we think of hotly contested issues such as abortion
rights, economic inequality, the question of legalizing euthanasia, and
so on. As mentioned earlier, Hong and Page assume a homogeneity of
values among decision makers. That is, everyone has the same overall

aim when making a decision. We have good reason to think that this might not be the case in the real world, and that, instead of value homogeneity, we are actually dealing with value diversity. The first problem this causes is in terms of how deliberators will evaluate the options in front of them—that is, are they interested in the same outcome? Will they all measure the validity of a proposal in the same way, with the same metric? This is an important assumption in terms of how the deliberative process functions, as it will ensure that deliberators all recognize the same things as resulting in a better outcome. Moreover, if there is disagreement on this question of what a better solution will even look like, this will likely prevent deliberators from recognizing an improvement when they are confronted with one, which in turn can prematurely halt the deliberative process as a whole.[64] Finally, even in cases where seemingly core values are shared among large numbers of people, we cannot be sure that they will all weigh them in an equivalent way. That is, although people might share agreement about the importance of some value, for some of them this might be outweighed by a further unshared value that takes precedence.[65]

The theorems put forward by Hong and Page also work on the assumption that knowledge is equally distributed among the relevant group—a situation of epistemic equality—but, in the real world, we know that this is not the case. Like it or not, there are such things as experts. I, for example, probably know more about regression models and the San Francisco Giants baseball team than the average British citizen. Similarly, and of more practical use, medical doctors know more about how our internal organs function than the rest of us. Missing from existing discussions on the likely epistemic benefits of a cognitively diverse group of political decision makers is how to integrate expert opinion into the decision-making process. For example, it is clear that decision makers will want to hear the opinions of various kinds of stakeholders in a given decision area, but existing accounts are not clear either how it will be decided who counts as an 'expert', something that is rarely uncontentious, or how much weight their opinion should be given. As the political theorist Alfred Moore writes, 'Politics is a domain in which we come to agreement about who the experts are and how far we can trust them, and how their judgment is to be integrated into the wider production of democratic will'.[66] Deciding the role of experts would be an important step if we were to look to maximize cognitive diversity in political institutions, and this itself would be a political decision. As Matt Sleat tells us, politics comes in when we are in the 'position of not only disagreeing what to do but of disagreeing as to the right justifications and considerations that ought to bear on the decision about how we ought to collectively proceed'.[67]

Aside from the theoretical issues noted above, a more empirical objection is that the kind of information citizens bring to the decision-making table, particularly their apparently poor levels of political knowledge, really does matter and cannot be fixed post hoc by deliberation or any of the other mechanisms described above. As computer scientists are fond of saying, this might be a case of 'junk in, junk out', or as the political theorist Paul Gunn puts it, 'Aggregating and deliberating about poor information is no substitute for good information'.[68] Specifically, it isn't entirely clear how deliberation between large numbers of individuals with factually incorrect or irrelevant information will produce a correct or good outcome, at least not without multiple stages of trial and error wherein potential solutions are enacted, fail, and are subsequently refined. Writing about this problem, Gunn expresses the fear that the 'intuitive' solution to a given problem, and thus the one around which most deliberators are likely to coalesce, is not obviously going to be the best, or even the correct, solution.[69] As such, if the instrumental benefits of democracy are the primary reason that you support it, it isn't clear on this reading why you would not look for a minimalist version of it that, on paper, appeared to offer some guaranteed epistemic benefits—that is, a democratized version of expert rule.[70]

So, where does this leave us? First, it seems that although there is definitely some kind of case to be made for diversity on epistemic grounds, it is not necessarily one that we should want to be the lynchpin of any argument. However, it is equally clear that it shouldn't be thrown out altogether. As discussed above, there is a growing body of case-study evidence that offers support for an instrumental case in broad sweeps, suggesting that although some of the theoretical assumptions required for it to hang together might seem odd on paper, they appear to come out in the wash when the principles are applied in the world. Second, this does nothing to reduce the power of the normative case in favour of having a more diverse political class. What it might do is simply underline that, although an instrumental argument might be more exciting or attractive right now, we should not lose sight of the intrinsic arguments that led us to be open to these other arguments in the first place. In reality, as we live our lives we consistently mix these approaches. Sometimes we are instrumentalist consequentialists, sometimes we are intrinsic-minded deontologists.[71] I don't see that we can't also keep two sets of books when thinking about why the composition of the political class matters.

A final point to address here is the question of whether, if we are more committed to the normative argument in favour of diversity than the argument focused on outcomes, does any outcome go? In other words, if we are bound to sticking with the most democratic procedure possible based on the moral force of the argument in its favour, are we unable to pass any judgement at all on the quality of the outcomes it produces? Critics such as Jason Brennan suggest that pure proceduralism is immoral on these grounds and that it can leave us in the position of condoning any outcome simply because we are supportive of the procedure that generated it. Although a pure form of proceduralism might be guilty of this, it seems to me that this is a caricature of the position held by many who write on this question. An obvious response to this line of questioning is simply to assert that a minimal framework for assessing outcomes could be constructed using the same values that inform the development of the procedure. So, as democratic procedures are initiated in a spirit of equality and human dignity, we would be able to criticize, or potentially neither recognize nor obey, democratic outcomes that flagrantly inhibit either or both of these principles, certainly in more marginal and extreme cases, on the same grounds.[72]

Conclusion: Reframing the Political-Class Issue as One of (In)equality and Effectiveness

The major takeaway from this chapter is that the epistemic defence of an unrepresentative and non-diverse political class put forward in Chapter 2 is built on flimsy theoretical and empirical evidence. Critically, the characterization of politics required for such a position to remain standing is limited and does not hold up well under scrutiny. Politics is a collective endeavour in which we confront the unknown together, almost always disagreeing about what doing this should entail. It is not a purely bureaucratic exercise in evidence-based implementation. Political knowledge cannot be classified solely as the rote memorization of facts of dubious relevance. Empirically, there is a growing body of work that suggests diversity might not be the disaster sceptics expect it to be. Although conceptual confusions preclude a full-throated endorsement of this work here, it should give us pause for thought when we hear the next person content to simply write off the political utility of the knowledge possessed by all of us in some way.

The tension between the intrinsic and instrumental defences runs beyond the question of moral primacy when diagnosing the problem and into the realm of how best to actually address the problem itself. If your main concern with a non-diverse political class is that it is unfair, your views as to what an acceptable remedy for this may be will differ from those of someone whose worries instead centre on the non-maximization of potential epistemic benefits that might be gained from having a more diverse set of politicians. To put it another way, depending on what you think the worst element of the problem itself is, you will have a different view as to what should be done to resolve it, and as to whether representative distortions of any kind are permissible. A further potential concern for those who are convinced of the likely epistemic benefits of a diverse political class is that of feasibility—exactly how can these tenets be applied to a real-world country of over 60 million people? Squaring this and the other circles identified above is the work of the next chapter.

4

How to Make the Political Class More Diverse

So far, this book has made the case that a more diverse political class is both intrinsically and potentially instrumentally desirable. Greater diversity, I argued, not only better fulfils democratic ideals of political equality and justice, but it may even bring further instrumental benefits. The diagnosis of the ill, therefore, is clear. In this chapter, I turn to the medicine, the question of how to actually bring about greater diversity. What concrete things can be done to get a more diverse group of people into political institutions?

As I noted at the close of the previous chapter, the main concern you have with the non-diverse status quo will likely be reflected in your preferred potential solution. The distinction between those concerned with justice and those preoccupied with epistemic or instrumental concerns is reflected in the general structure of the chapter. I begin by considering possible diversity-increasing methods that can take place within the political apparatus we have now, that of holding elections to choose representatives. I discuss the kinds of barriers that currently stand in the way of greater diversity in the political class and broadly identify two kinds.[1] The first are social barriers, relating to constructed norms and arrangements in society that result in certain individuals being less likely than others to consider running for office. Second, and perhaps more controversial, are non-social barriers, such as individual personality traits and other dispositions that evidence suggests are genetic in origin. Building on this second area, I reflect on what kinds of biases or sources of unrepresentativeness, if any, might ever be acceptable, and ask whether there are limits to the effectiveness of the policy proposals I outline. Broadly, these solutions will primarily rectify the ill of injustice, making the political class more diverse in certain ways, but they will not necessarily bring about the instrumental epistemic benefits discussed earlier or break apart the underlying social structures that result in systematic under-representation of certain groups in the first instance.[2]

I then consider more radical proposals for increasing diversity among the political class, most notably eschewing the electoral method of selecting representatives in favour of a system of random selection by lot. These reforms would be designed to maximize the cognitive diversity we are told is necessary to reap in full the available epistemic rewards and to bypass entirely social inequalities that result in the skewed presence of some groups in political institutions.

Supply and Demand in Political Recruitment

In electoral democracies, prospective candidates put themselves forward for election, generally under the banner of a political party, and then seek to gain more votes than their opponents. In such a system of electoral competition, the onus is on individuals to step into the political arena. The dominant framework for thinking about political recruitment, the process by which individuals become political candidates and possibly elected politicians, is that of supply and demand. First used to describe the process of candidate selection in the 1990s by Pippa Norris and Joni Lovenduski, the framework borrows economic terminology to distinguish between two kinds of variable that can help us explain the unrepresentative composition of political institutions. Supply-side factors are those that focus on the flow of people coming forward as potential candidates. For example, a supply-side explanation for the low numbers of women in a given political institution would highlight the fact that a lower number of women than men expressed an interest in the available candidacies. Demand-side factors do the opposite and look to the political actors already in place, arguing that in their role as the gatekeepers of political office they have preferences for certain kinds of candidates over others. Returning to the example of low numbers of women in political institutions, a demand-side explanation would see this as a result of political parties not wanting women to come forward as candidates, or not selecting them when they did.

The supply-and-demand framework has been made to carry a lot of weight in academic work over the last twenty years, with various additions and revisions being suggested. Overall, though, it still stands up and brings order to our thinking about a complex process.[3] As I will discuss below, most of the influences identified as playing a role in political recruitment reach across the divide between supply and demand. This was anticipated by Norris and Lovenduski, who refer to a 'feedback loop' between the two. How so? Take the example of the demand-side factor mentioned above, that of a political party not selecting those women who put themselves forward as potential candidates. At first look, this is a clear issue of demand: simply, the party is actively expressing no demand for women candidates. However, it is equally plausible that there is an added supply-side effect to this, whereby women in the population might witness the lack of demand and then think it is not worth considering a candidacy themselves. This then reinforces the reasoning behind the party holding their initial view ('why bother if women are not interested?'), and so on ad infinitum.

How Political Parties Could Make the Political Class More Diverse

If you want to be a politician in Britain right now, the first decision you face is for which party.[4] For better or worse, political parties are the primary, if not quite the sole, provider of our political operatives. Despite a handful of notable exceptions in most democracies, nearly every politician you have ever heard of will have been affiliated to a political party of some kind. Why are parties so dominant? To a large extent it is because they have the resources and infrastructure to organize large numbers of candidacies across a given polity. They will offer a candidate a ready-to-go campaign team, a manifesto, volunteers, posters, recognizable typefaces, and so on. Of course, for a candidate these things are useful. Not only does this save candidates organizing such things for themselves, it also gives them a heuristic, or reputational shortcut, with which they can appeal to voters who will recognize the party's stable traits and who may even already have positive feelings towards them. In short, parties are the main vehicle that can transform private citizens into public politicians due to their infrastructure and existing dominance of political life. This makes them extremely powerful, and for this reason it is no overstatement to suggest that parties can either make or break attempts to achieve greater diversity among political candidates and elected politicians. In this section, I will review the research undertaken on the question of how parties might aid this process, and ask what has happened when they have tried to do this in the past.

Sarah Childs and her colleagues identify three levels of commitment that a party might make to increasing diversity among candidates (in the case they discuss, increasing the numbers of women). They distinguish between equality rhetoric, equality promotion, and equality guarantees. As the names suggest, these measures move from weak to something somewhat stronger and are defined in greater detail in Table 4.1.

So, what kinds of things can parties do? Thinking again in terms of supply and demand, political parties have large amounts of direct control over the latter and, indirectly, a significant measure of influence over the former. If political parties at large are the macro-level gatekeepers of political life, effectively deciding who may or may not be an electoral candidate, the individuals who are directly involved in selecting candidates in each constituency are the micro-level gatekeepers. Political scientists refer to these people as party 'selectorates'—a portmanteau word combining selectors and electorate that reflects their function. Historically, research has made the case that these selectorates can be biased against women, ethnic minorities, LGBT, or other prospective candidates who do not fit the 'traditional' mould of a political candidate, which was something like a professional white man, married with children. Often, such dubious selection practices have taken place

Table 4.1 Definitions of different equality-seeking strategies available to political parties, adapted from Childs et al. (2005).[5]

Rhetoric	Promotion	Guarantees
Public acceptance of claims for representation.	Attempts to bring those who are currently under-represented into political competition.	Requires an increase in the number or proportion of particular candidates; makes a particular social characteristic a necessary qualification for office.

under the veneer of meritocracy, an idea often used in defence of current patterns in political recruitment. I discuss meritocracy further below, and offer a critique of it as part of a broader defence of quotas. For now, consider the idea of meritocracy to be one which states that the only relevant characteristic in selecting politicians is their apparent acumen as regards the job, something which advocates of meritocracy claim can be assessed objectively by those selecting from a group of aspiring candidates in spite of its conceptual fluidity and likely incoherence. Consequently, when seeking to generate a more diverse group of candidates, political parties have had to face up to these challenges and sought to intervene in the selection process by disrupting the traditional methods and composition of selectorates in various ways.

The simplest thing that parties can do is to publicly acknowledge the need to attract a more diverse group of prospective candidates. This strategy, one of voicing equality-promoting rhetoric, is certainly the easiest thing for parties to do in terms of administration and set-up, even though it might call for the use of political capital all the same. Rhetoric focused on the need for equality is common, with essentially all the major political parties in the UK subscribing to the idea. Such utterances can now be heard from much of the ideological spectrum of British political life. Compare the following quotes from the (then) political leaders of the two main parties:

We will change the way we look.... We need to change the scandalous under representation of women....[6]

And we need a politics where politicians look like the constituents they represent. That's not what Westminster looks like today.[7]

The first quote is from a speech by David Cameron of the Conservative Party, the second by Ed Miliband of the Labour Party, but the underlying premise of both is all but identical—diversity, in this case identity diversity in the form of descriptive representation, matters. Moving beyond simply employing rhetoric espousing the benefits of greater diversity, parties can undertake activities and make other moves that actively promote it. A major intervention in the candidate selection process by political parties has come in the form of open primaries. As opposed to guaranteeing an outcome by manipulating the candidate pool to ensure commonality in terms of the desired characteristics such as sex or ethnicity, the adoption of an open primary is an attempt to enlarge the selectorate itself in the hope that a 'more representative' group may think differently, and thus select differently, from the traditional smaller group. As such, open primary adoption lies some-where between equality rhetoric and equality promotion, offering no guarantee as to the outcome of the selection process. In the UK, this approach has been used most prominently by the Conservative Party, with recent research putting the number of primaries used by the party since 2003 in the 'hundreds'.[8] However, whether or not the primaries had the transformative effect on both participation and selection that their architects desired is debatable. Some academics, drawing on interviews with candidates in constituencies that held primaries, have suggested that there were 'very thin boundaries between the different categories of the selectorate that is voters, supporters and members' and that 'supporters actually form the bulk of the voters who eventually turn out at primary meetings'.[9] Despite this uncertainty, it has been the case that the Conservative parliamentary cohort has diversified during the period that primaries have occurred. What remains unclear is whether this is actually a causal relationship.

In addition, parties may also seek to alter the selection process with other, lighter-touch measures that still move beyond rhetoric alone— those of equality promotion. These include introducing diversity-focused training for members of selection panels and adjusting the protocols for the process of interviewing candidates at the local level.[10] Looking again at examples of this in the UK, the Conservatives, not adopting a full gender quota, sought to implement a system by which the central party would pre-approve candidates who could then be shortlisted by individual constituencies. Referred to as the 'priority list' or the 'A-list' and implemented on the watch of the then newly elected leader of the party, David Cameron, the system was designed to nudge constituency associations to shortlist a more diverse group of candidates. Again, its impact is considered to have been fairly small.[11]

Another thing that parties can do is deceptively simple: they can ask people from traditionally under-represented groups to consider putting themselves forward for candidacy. A consistent finding across existing research is that 'having been asked to run [is] the modal explanation for candidacy or the factor most positively associated with interest in running'.[12] Of course, the point of interest here is, who is being asked? If party figures are simply asking people who are like themselves to consider a candidacy, the chances are that this kind of recruitment will not fundamentally change the composition of political institutions. If focused specifically on groups that are traditionally under-represented, however, it might cause fundamental change; though if membership of such a group generally correlates with scarcity in other kinds of resources necessary to running for office, the positive effect might be muted somewhat.

Finally, we come to equality guarantees, which generally take the form of a quota of some kind. In the UK, the only political party to adopt a gender quota for parliamentary candidate selections is the Labour Party. The all-women shortlist (AWS) policy was adopted by the party a few years ahead of the 1997 general election, but it was dropped in 1996 following a legal challenge by party members who felt it infringed on their right to put themselves forward as candidates. Tony Blair reintroduced the policy in 2001, this time making it fully legal thanks to changes made subsequently to the 2002 Sex Discrimination (Election Candidates) Act. AWS essentially does what the name suggests it will, ensuring that all candidates on a shortlist in a given constituency are women, making it impossible for the candidate selected for the party in that constituency to be anything other than a woman. This is, in the framework of Childs and her colleagues, an equality guarantee, which leaves nothing to chance. The policy worked, and the number of women in the House of Commons doubled overnight at the 1997 general election, almost entirely thanks to AWS. This kind of success has been replicated worldwide, and it is now generally accepted among scholars that gender quotas increase the numbers of women in politics across the board,[13] though there is some discussion as to whether this is dependent on the type of quota that is adopted.[14] I offer an in-principle defence of quotas below, but for now suffice it to say that quota policies, although controversial, appear to bring about their intended outcome more often than not.

Of course, quotas of any kind require a generally clear categorization of the characteristics to which the quota is being applied in order to function smoothly. For example, quotas focused on sex are mostly dispute-free on this front because the distinction between men and women is relatively clear in practice.[15] Similarly, in other parts of the world quotas in the form of reserved seats for certain ethnic minorities work on the basis that membership of the group can be demonstrated reasonably straightforwardly. It is, however, easy to see how this kind of clean delineation will not apply in all cases, something that limits the extent to which quota adoption will bring about the wholesale diversification of the political class. Think about social class, for example. If we accept the argument that we should have more politicians from working-class backgrounds, and that quotas would probably be the quickest way to implement this within the constraints of an electoral selection method, we need to know what distinguishes a working-class candidate from other candidates. Would it be occupation, income, accent, parental occupation during the candidate's early life, or any or all of these things in combination? It is very difficult to identify the pivotal characteristic with any certainty. This is not to say that the only response to this difficulty is to throw our hands up and leave things as they are, but it makes clear the tricky mechanics involved in the process of getting such a quota off the ground.[16]

A Defence of Quotas of All Kinds

As noted, it appears that the quickest electoral fix to many of the problems discussed in this book is to subvert the existing processes by which political candidates are selected through the use of quotas.

Quotas, however, are not popular. As the political philosopher Elizabeth Anderson observes, 'Bureaucracy offers a way out of many inegalitarian ills, but it is expensive medicine to obtain, and hard to administer to recalcitrant patients'.[17] The standard argument against quotas claims that they are unfair, introducing a previously absent and apparently irrelevant qualification into the job description of a political candidate—either being a women or from a specific ethnic minority in most cases seen to date.[18] As a result, critics claim, quotas destroy what was previously a meritocratic system and exclude those individuals who, aside from being the wrong sex or having the wrong ethnicity, would otherwise be excellent candidates for office. This gives the 'quota' candidates an easier ride, we are told. Consequently, candidates selected via a quota are claimed to be of lower quality than their colleagues selected through traditional channels. Empirically, various studies of quotas for women have shown the latter claim to be false, with women selected and elected through quotas appearing actually to be roughly the same as men in terms of all feasibly relevant experience and behaviour. For example, in a study I conducted with David Cutts and Rosie Campbell that compared women elected in 1997 via Labour's all-women shortlist policy with their colleagues, we found no differences between 'quota women' and everyone else. In fact, we found some evidence that might lead these women to be considered more qualified than the candidates elected via the traditional process.[19] Rainbow Murray uncovered similar patterns in France, a country which has already inserted a clause in its constitution committing it to the pursuit of gender parity in legislative composition.[20] In short, existing studies confirm that quotas do not appear to have any negative effect on the way that assemblies function and do not result in lower-quality candidates as measured by traditional metrics.

Above and beyond this, however, there is a strong refutation to be made of the argument that quotas are unfair regardless of whether they have any of the above effects. As I have argued throughout the book, we cannot cash out the potential benefits that quotas might have solely in terms of consequences relating to candidates' supposed 'quality', or their rate of legislative activity, or similar. Research has discussed how, in cases where gender quotas are adopted that ensure the selection of a woman in a given constituency, opponents characterize it as limiting the freedoms and rights of men who were keen to run, and is therefore itself also unfair. The opponents see the situation as one in which one form of unfairness has met an equivalent other form. However, there are arguably sleights of hand at work in this argument.

The sleights of hand relate primarily to the nature of the comparison being made. Although I do not wish to underestimate the disappointment an individual man might feel in a single instance of not being able to run for parliamentary candidacy in his local constituency, should it be selected as a quota seat, the idea that this is equivalent to the chronic under-representation of women in political institutions seems slightly fantastic. Assuming that one accepts the idea that quotas are being used to correct for ongoing patterns of sexist discrimination, it is hard to see how the case can simultaneously be made that these are equivalent injustices. A further misdirection causes us to focus our attention on one level of analysis in place of another. By this I refer to the way in which the debate is sculpted to become one about an individual man's right to stand in a given constituency of his choice. Understandably, we are prone to empathize with stories of hard-working local party men whose candidacies perish under the wheels of the approaching quota, and thus we are potentially equally prone to see the women being allowed to stand in his stead as somehow less authentic or worthy of the job. The psychologist Paul Bloom writes: 'Empathy is like a spotlight directing attention...but spotlights have a narrow focus...spotlights only illuminate what they are pointed at.'[21] As I mentioned above, the claim that 'quality' drops when quotas are introduced does not hold empirically. However, I think there is a further point to be made in the discussion about quotas that forces us to address the deeper question about what we want our political institutions to be and what we want them to do.

Implicit in the move to adopt quotas is the endorsement of a set of normative ideas about the purpose of politics and political institutions. Throughout this book I have argued in favour of a kind of institutional politics that allows for a changing and more diverse group of citizens to play a role in political decision-making. As discussed earlier, in formal terms it is possible to make the case that we already have a system that facilitates the fruition of such a vision in the sense that the majority of adults, with relatively few exceptions, have the legal right to put themselves forward as candidates in legislative elections. This is not something I dispute. However, the evidence laid out in Chapter 1 shows quite clearly that most people are not exercising this right. Those who are appear to be concentrated in sections of society, suggesting that broader social inequalities are driving this imbalance, and that it is these inequalities that affect individuals' capacity and willingness to use the formal right that they have had all along. If we are to achieve greater diversity in our political class while maintaining a system of election, we would do well to think more carefully about how to negate those distortions that result in some individuals leaving their formal right to participate in public life to gather dust, unused. More than this, we should also consider, along the lines mentioned in the previous chapter, why this might matter for all of us in a collective sense.

So, how to negate these influences? Broadly, there are two options here, which might be seen as the best answer and a good answer, respectively.[22] The first would be to eradicate the social inequalities driving these patterns; these include economic inequality, class prejudice, racism, sexism, and geographic inequalities in various resources that influence the likelihood of someone running for political office. Although many are invested in the pursuit of this goal, it seems unlikely to be achieved any time soon, if ever. The philosopher Jeffrey Green argues, quite convincingly, that the pernicious effect of personal wealth on the propensity to participate in politics is probably inescapable so long as a liberal commitment to the institutions of both the family and private property is maintained.[23] In short, if we are serious about altering the composition of the political class, assuming that change will come of its own accord is misguided.

This is where the second option, in the form of quotas, comes in. Instead of waiting for the slow work of wholesale social progress to take hold, or indeed accepting that there will be limits to what social changes might ever be brought about, quotas of various kinds artificially create instances of conditions in which these inequalities are rendered temporarily irrelevant, allowing them to be circumvented and overcome in the artificially egalitarian space created by the quota.[24]

Quotas are not ideal. For one thing, as discussed earlier, their application is limited to cases where the relevant characteristic can be easily identified. Even where this is the case, there are further issues. Do gender quotas, for example, infringe on the formal rights of a certain number of men when they are utilized? They probably do, though only temporarily and in geographically delimited areas. Does this mean we should not use them? I do not think that it does. We can think about quotas, and any endorsement of their adoption, as a signal of approval for a certain set of goals for political institutions and political culture, which their adoption is presumed to aid. Quotas can be justified on these terms. These goals would be something akin to what the philosopher Michael Sandel calls the 'public philosophy' that lies behind the conduct of public life as a whole.[25] Sandel famously espouses a variant of the republican conception of freedom that 'cultivates in citizens the qualities of character self-government requires'.[26] As he points out, this means that such a conception of freedom is not value-free, nor does it claim to be. It actively and explicitly wants to promote these values among citizens. This allows the republican notion of political participation to extend beyond the more limited liberal idea that one may choose to participate if one wishes. Reflecting on the sense of disengagement he sees as permeating American democratic life in the twenty-first century, Sandel writes:

If American politics is to revitalize the civic strand of freedom, it must find a way to ask what economic arrangements are hospitable to self-government, and how the public life of a pluralist society might cultivate in citizens the expansive self-understandings that civic engagement requires.[27]

I do not necessarily endorse Sandel's exact position here, but I think he is correct that seriously thinking about the causes and circumstances of widespread political disconnect and disengagement means asking questions about societal structures as a whole and, critically, thinking more explicitly about what we want our political institutions to look like, and what we want them to do.[28] To put it another way, adopting quotas of any kind is emblematic of an acknowledgement of the fact both that existing social and economic inequalities are clearly limiting the participation of certain groups of society, and that this is something of concern.

Along similarly questioning lines that could also be used to justify the use of quotas, the political philosopher Suzanne Dovi has defended the role of exclusion in ensuring that democratic practices live up to their name.[29] She suggests that we adopt what she calls a 'perspective of exclusion' and think about how limiting the political influence of certain powerful individuals and groups will actually make democracy work better, at least in the sense of living up to principles of political equality. She sees this as especially true when attempting to rectify historical imbalances of political power, such as in cases where societal groups were previously formally barred from participating in processes of political decision-making. Why so? Partly, she argues, because even in the absence of formal barriers to participation for these groups, informal barriers will persist, as will the long-standing power of the previously dominant group, often embedded in the very design and workings of assemblies and other political structures themselves. Their power is, so to speak, to be found right there in the bricks. Noting that this is relatively unacknowledged in existing research on descriptive representation, she writes that 'this omission is troubling because the adequate representation of historically disadvantaged groups may require those who occupy relationships of privilege to shut up, recuse themselves, or even resign coveted positions of power in order to create space for disadvantaged groups'.[30] In other words, ensuring that increasing inclusion functions in a democratic way will sometimes require us to attend to exclusion, albeit in temporary and non-formal ways.[31] This is especially important if the inequalities that generate exclusion are unlikely to die off naturally, or at all.

The above debate about quotas shines light on the largely implicit assumptions inherent in the positions generally taken on the issue.

Endorsing quotas is also about endorsing the idea that our open and democratic political system does not simply exist as a vehicle for individual fulfilment.[32] Instead, it is about making collective decisions as a political community, and deciding that we need quotas to better do this is also a statement about who within that community can, and should, be making those decisions. This is not to say that I think those who object to quotas are evil or misguided and need to be educated to the point of acquiescence. However, it is important to make clear the normative vision of politics that is inherent in such a position. People are perfectly entitled to argue against quotas, but in doing so they need to defend their own notions of what political institutions are for and account for the likely implications of the position they endorse. The idea that the existing system, producing roughly the same kind of politician for over a hundred years, was truly meritocratic seems unlikely. As with any such claim, a good test is to see if there are the same winners and losers each time. If there are, it probably is not meritocratic, or at least not as meritocratic as it purports to be. Another possible retort here is that under-represented groups, such as women or members of ethnic minorities, have freely chosen not to run for office and that we should respect their agency. Anne Phillips, anticipating such an objection, compares the feasibility of this preference explanation for group outcomes as opposed to individual outcomes:

When dealing with social groups, [individual] variations are more easily averaged out, and it becomes inherently suspicious to attribute systematic differences in outcome to the different mind-sets of different groups: this begs too many questions about why the members of one group might have ended up with a radically different set of preferences to another; and overlooks much we already know about the different conditions under which their choices were made.[33]

In other words, one's credulity in this matter would need to be stretched beyond the point of no return in order to sustain support for any objection based on supposed variations in group preferences.

Most of the potential diversity-promoting policies and strategies I have discussed so far focus on the individual candidate as the potential arena of change. In other words, they try to get individuals to run, or to get individual candidates on a shortlist. Other strategies have been suggested that instead look to the institutional context in which all of this takes place—for example, what the job of being a politician is actually like, or what the culture of political institutions implicitly says about them. It is to these suggestions I now turn.

Making Being a Politician More Compatible with Being a 'Normal Person'

In her paper titled 'The Costs of Tragedy', the political philosopher Martha Nussbaum describes those situations in life when we are presented with a decision that is not only difficult to resolve, but additionally 'all the possible answers to [this] question... are bad, involving serious moral wrongdoing'.[34] The tragedy is that although we might be able to decide between one option and another, all the potential options we could have chosen would have involved us committing, or bringing about in some other way, an immoral act. So, for example, we might find ourselves in a war situation where any decision we make will result in loss of life, or perhaps in one of the myriad trolley-problem scenarios dreamt up to entertain philosophy undergraduates.

Far from being just a fanciful thought experiment, I think this argument has application to the situation faced by many individuals when choosing whether or not to run for political office. Imagine that Angela is considering running for political office. She is interested in politics, has a strong background of campaigning for her party, and genuinely feels that she will be able to give a voice to many of the people living in poverty in her neighbourhood. In short, she thinks she would do a lot of good for others, and alleviate much suffering, were she to run for office and become an elected politician.[35] However, Angela is also mother to two young children under the age of 10. Although she knows that her partner has a flexible job that would allow him to care for their children on many occasions during the working week, and that they have the financial resources to fund childcare for the rest of time, she feels acutely that her running for office would in some way deprive the children of important and worthy childhood experiences. This being the case, she is presented with a difficult decision: do the benefits of running for office outweigh the familial costs? But as Nussbaum's argument suggests, this is not the totality of the conundrum. The other possible options that Angela has in front of her are equally unsatisfactory. Does she recuse herself from politics altogether and spend all of her time with her children? Maybe she could, but she firmly believes that this would result in her not being able to alleviate the harm she would have been able to if she had become a politician. In effect, she would not be actively reducing harm. In the words of Nussbaum, all of the possible choices that Angela has seem to 'involve neglect of some important obligation', in this case either negatively impacting on her children in some way, or neglecting the needy prospective constituents she wants to help.[36] On Nussbaum's view, this is a tragic question to be faced with.

The point of raising Nussbaum's example is not to provoke readers' moral outrage regarding the proper role of women in society—Angela might just as easily have been Tony, Nigel, or Walter. The children might instead have been ageing parents or a sick spouse. Wanting to help the impoverished could be replaced by simply wanting to achieve some long-held personal desire or life goal. Regardless, the tragic question still rears its head in all of these cases. The effect that Nussbaum's argument really has is to highlight our agency in these matters: we have the ability to redesign circumstances that appear to continually give rise to specific cases of the tragic question in ways that mean they will not be doomed to do this indefinitely. In the practical terms of the above example, the question is how can we make the role of being an elected politician, and the process by which an individual becomes one, more compatible with the wide range of obligations that almost all of us have to some extent as we go through life?[37] That is, we can come to the realization that there are things we can do to make the job of being a politician more suited to the lives of 'normal people'. As Nussbaum writes, we should take note that 'many tragedies are produced not by natural necessity or by anything about the character of the contending values, but simply by habit and tradition, treated as natural and inevitable'.[38]

Right now, being an MP is a tough sell, with long and irregular hours that are difficult to combine with the domestic caring duties undertaken by large numbers of the population. Many people who may otherwise have some interest in taking the job on, and are mulling over a candidacy, might be put off by thoughts of the inauspicious reality in which they would likely find themselves. They would be Angela, and they would be faced with a tragic decision. So, what should we do to help them?

As I write this, I can already envisage some people responding, 'nothing'. Their argument will proceed, I imagine, that we should only want people in our political institutions who *really* want to be there, who have sacrificed something in pursuit of office. On the face of it, this seems a perfectly reasonable statement that we would rush to endorse. But on reflection, it is clearly based on the flawed premise that everyone is equally able to demonstrate this desire in the traditional currency discussed earlier—things like time and other social and financial resources. I hope I have established by now that this is not the case. Further, and to reinforce Nussbaum's point, such opposition assumes that the presence of this kind of trade-off is inevitable, treating the status quo in terms of how politicians are expected to work and live as somehow immutable. This is a fallacious assumption.

There are multiple options available to the willing reformer, some more resource-intensive, and perhaps even revolutionary, than others. The least controversial suggestions focus on making political institutions more 'family-friendly', a phrase often used euphemistically in place of 'woman-friendly'.[39] The suggestions include, but are not limited to, ensuring the availability of parental leave for legislators, implementing flexible working patterns that reflect school holidays and daily domestic routines, reducing the frequency of late-night legislative sessions in the institution, introducing flexible working for politicians who are also carers, and having a crèche on site.[40] Although these suggestions might sound quite tame, they have been hotly disputed. Some critics have seen appeals for a reduction in sitting hours to be reflective of MPs' inherent laziness, or indeed their preference to be out gallivanting of an evening rather than working. More reflective critics have acknowledged that there is a trade-off to be made when implementing certain changes. If daily sitting hours were reduced, those MPs whose constituencies are further from Westminster (or wherever the assembly in question is based) would need to spend more of the week in London. Conversely, staying late and cramming their hours into fewer days means they can escape the city a day or two earlier and return to their constituencies. A more radical option is that of job-sharing, whereby two MPs would share the duties of representing a single constituency, either splitting the hours of the job in half, or equitably dividing the associated responsibilities in some other way. Research by Rosie Campbell and Philip Cowley suggests that the public are fairly indifferent to this option, expressing neither great support for nor significant opposition to it, even when the rationale behind adopting such a system is explained to them.[41]

In July 2016, Sarah Childs published a report on these and other related issues entitled *The Good Parliament*. Her suggestions, most of which could apply to many well-established political institutions, include enforcing a code of conduct for MPs when inside the House of Commons chamber, allowing MPs to bend the existing rules in such a way that they could vote in the Commons whilst remaining with their children (something they cannot currently do), introducing sex quotas for the election of committee chairs, and, in what has proved to be the most controversial suggestion, allowing female MPs to breastfeed their young children in the House of Commons chamber.[42] Criticism of the final proposal has focused on the fact that breastfeeding would not be allowed in a professional business setting seen as comparable to Parliament—the newsroom at a media organization, for example—and therefore MPs should not be given this special privilege.[43] Of course, as Childs has pointed out, this assumes that Parliament is bound by the existing conventions of business as opposed to being in the unique position of having the ability, and opportunity, to break out of them. This is part of a bigger point to be made about comparisons between Parliament, MPs, and the country at large. Take the complaint about MPs' working hours, for example. Many critics might say something to the effect of 'suck it up—the rest of us do'. There is something in this argument. Apparent special treatment for people who already seem rather well fed and watered is difficult to swallow. However, as I hope I have at least begun to convince you, extrapolating from this that we must, therefore, participate in a dismal race to the bottom, is wrong-headed. If we think of politics as an arena of individual fulfilment, this argument might make sense, but if we instead think of it as a collective endeavour by which we are all affected, it loses its shine.

As we have seen, many people and political parties now agree that the social biases I listed are unacceptable. Such biases rely on prejudice against individuals with certain characteristics that have no obvious effect on their ability to discharge the duties of the office they seek. Indeed, evidence suggests that they perform in these roles as well as anybody else. However, if it were ever to be the case that these prejudices were dealt with in such a way that made them redundant forces, would it be fine at this point to consider the job done? Probably not, as we will see in the next section.

The Limits of Social Intervention

Many commentators have contended that the aggressive and confrontational nature of legislative debate, such as that seen at PMQs in the House of Commons, is likely to be off-putting to those who do not feel they would perform well in such an environment. Academics have suggested that this group is likely to include women, given that women's voices are less likely to carry (even when amplified) across a rowdy legislative chamber. This is undoubtedly true. However, beyond changing these surface-level behaviours, I do not see these kinds of procedural reforms making a significant broader impact on the composition of the political class. Although a ban on shouting or jeering in the chamber might result in a more pleasant environment in which politicians can speak and be questioned, it would do nothing to alter the fundamental fact that politics is all about conflict. As discussed in the previous chapter, if there was no conflict, there would be no need for politics. A consequence of this is that the kinds of people willing to put themselves forward for political candidacy in the first place are more likely than not also going to be the kinds of people who deal well with sustained interpersonal conflict.

This is where we brush up against the limits of social influences, and where seeking a truly diverse political class without changing certain aspects of political life generally seen as fundamental, namely that we choose our representatives through open elections, is difficult. Fascinating research by members of the University of Nebraska–Lincoln's Political Physiology Lab offers biological evidence in support of the idea that some people might be better built for politics, and the conflict it entails, than others.[44] Taking a representative sample of voters, Jeffrey French and his colleagues found that the propensity of an individual to turn out to vote at repeated elections was positively correlated with their baseline cortisol levels. Cortisol, which can be measured in saliva, is reflective of how the neuroendocrine stress system, known as the hypothalamic–pituitary–adrenal (HPA) axis, of an individual is functioning. In plain terms, people who had high baseline cortisol levels were less likely to have voted in the previous five elections. Those with low baseline cortisol levels were more likely to have voted. These effects held even when taking into account canonical social predictors of voting, such as age and level of education. The finding suggests that people who deal well with stress at the biological level are more likely to participate in the kinds of political activity involving 'decision-making and emotional conflict among potentially politically incompatible alternatives'.[45] This could just as easily be a description of what it must be like to be an MP, or more clearly, a politician in the party leadership.

Recent research in political science has also explored the role of personality traits in shaping political behaviour. A consistent finding has been that individuals who generally prefer to avoid conflict in their life, something found in their personality traits and behaviour, are less likely to involve themselves in political activities than those who do not share these traits. So, for example, individuals who score highly on measures of how extroverted or open to new experiences they are tend to find political participation more attractive overall, but especially those types of participation that involve being out in the world and meeting new people.[46] Examples of this might include campaigning in their neighbourhood, attending a rally, or, presumably, putting themselves forward for public office.

Taken together, these research findings make intuitive sense. If I am more shy than my brother, or my cousin is far more outgoing than me, both of them are probably more likely to want to compete for a job that involves having one's face plastered on posters, one's sex life discussed on the Internet, or that requires meeting anything from a hundred to a hundred thousand prospective voters across a campaign. Simply, some of us might be built for this in ways that others are not. Hypothetically, we might end up in a situation where, having successfully removed all traces of social bias from political life (sexism, racism, ageism, and so on), we replace this with a new political class of extremely confident, somewhat aggressive, and highly extroverted individuals. Would these kinds of differences matter for reasons of justice (ensuring equality of access to the institutions) and for instrumental reasons (in terms of the decisions the legislature makes)? I am agnostic on this point, but it seems to me that the instrumental question is more pertinent here given that personality traits do not seem to be, in and of themselves, requiring of political representation in the way that race and sex are, for example. It does, however, seem right to think that we might want a better mix of personality types in the assembly for reasons relating to the quality of its outputs. Aside from these concerns, is there anything we could feasibly do about this while continuing to choose our politicians by electing them?

There is evidence to suggest that there might be. We might consider ways in which we can reframe what it means to be a politician—that is, rethinking how we discuss the purpose of holding political office. As Monica Schneider and her colleagues have put it, 'ambition for *what*?'[47] In a recent study, they found that people in general saw the pursuit of a political career as intrinsically linked to 'power-related goals', such as promoting oneself and competing with others. Societal patterns of gendered socialization have been found to leave women 'predisposed to avoid conflict' and that this may lie behind 'the reticence of women to embrace activities associated with ... power goals'.[48] In other words, the fact that women, on average, have lower levels of political ambition than men might be dependent on how politics itself is defined and perceived.[49] The results of Schneider's study offer support for this notion, and she and her colleagues found that reframing the pursuit of a political career as being about caring for others, serving humanity as a whole, and working with others reduced the gap in political ambition between men and women in their sample. This suggests that reforming, or even simply reframing, the activity of politics as being a communal effort might reduce the extent to which it deters those who have personality traits consistent with avoiding conflict.

Political practice may not be immutable and could certainly be sanitized to a point. But the pursuit of power and its exercise undoubtedly lie at the core of politics. This being the case, it might be difficult to convince people who truly did not want to be involved to put themselves forward for election. Combating this barrier requires more radical thinking.

Why Randomly Selecting our Representatives Might Solve the Problem of the Political Class

As has become clear, it is difficult to harmonize the desire for greater diversity among political decision makers in a representative parliament with the mechanism we currently use to choose them—elections. Although it is possible for both demand- and supply-side factors to be manipulated or altered, certain obstacles to true diversity—psychological predispositions, for example, and more notably the overwhelming influence of social and economic inequality—persist. One solution is to use quotas and other measures that focus on increasing the descriptive representation of a single given characteristic considered to be politically relevant and desirable. However, political identities are rarely as simple as this—people are not defined by a sole characteristic, and the lives we live reflect this complexity. Although increasing diversity one characteristic at a time might be the simplest way to do it, it is unlikely, in the longer run, to result in the kind of true cognitive diversity discussed earlier. This is not to say that such diversity-seeking strategies are ineffective, as they have consistently been shown to have the desired effect. In some cases, such as those where a fairly well-defined societal group seek to increase their political representation as part of a campaign to redress specific historical injustices or inequalities, this is not a concern. Outside of these cases, though, and many of the issues at the heart of the political-class narrative do not fit this bill, the case could be made that measures focused on a single characteristic are a pragmatic solution that generally falls short of a more absolute standard of diversity.

My claim is that this is at least partly a result of the most common method by which our politicians are chosen—election. In this section I will discuss an alternative to the electoral mechanism for selecting representatives, that of randomly selecting by lot individuals who will serve in Parliament.

As with my argument for diversity among representatives as a whole, there is both a normative and an instrumental case to be made in favour of random selection. Normatively, the thought here is that random selection offers each eligible citizen an exactly equal chance of holding political power.[50] Instrumentally, there is a growing body of work making the case that the outcomes offered by random selection are potentially better than those offered by traditional elected representation.[51] I will address both in turn before very tentatively outlining some suggestions as to how such a system might function. As with the arguments for diversity discussed earlier, my view is that the matter is essentially a normative one and, although we might speculate as to the instrumental benefits, these should not take prominence.

In Chapter 1 I demonstrated how unrepresentative the current and historical occupants of the House of Commons have been of the wider population of the UK, with legislative composition reflecting wider inequality in social standing and relations. Those groups who sit at the sharp end of these unequal relations are present in far smaller numbers than those who sit at the opposite end. As noted by many, this suggests a strong connection between the workings of these social relations, things like relative economic poverty, sexism, and racism, and the likelihood that an individual who suffers the detrimental effects of these will consider running for political office, and thus potentially ever hold a position of significant political power. As I mentioned before, although most adults in society have the formal, legal right to put themselves forward as a political candidate, there are biases across the population that unequally distribute the likelihood of them doing so. In some sense strategies such as quotas seek to redistribute the characteristic or quality that allows individuals to take advantage of this right. But despite often doing this effectively, quotas leave untouched the social relation that produced the skewed distribution in the first place.[52] As such, quotas leave open the possibility, perhaps even the risk, that while they ameliorate the negative political impact of certain inequalities, the underlying unequal patterns, and others unaddressed by the specifics of the quota, remain intact. For example, a gender quota might leave patterns of class inequality and under-representation intact. This is not a reason *not* to implement them, but it should be known from the outset that quotas are not a universal solution in and of themselves. Along these lines, Elizabeth Anderson has suggested that egalitarian-minded individuals should 'reconceive equality as fundamentally a kind of social relationship rather than a pattern of distribution' and aim to end 'oppressive social relations (which are inherently relations of inequality)... realizing society conceived as a system of cooperation and affiliation among equals'.[53]

So, how does this relate to the composition of the political class? Instead of seeking to rectify inegalitarian imbalances after the event, what if the system itself did not allow for imbalances to be reflected in the political sphere in the first place? Alexander Guerrero has argued that 'although it may be true that all have an equal *say* in the electoral process, only a select few actually have political power, and (for reasons having to do with resources and the influence of the powerful) not everyone has anything close to an equal *chance* of having political power'.[54] Random selection changes this. No longer would any individual's chance of holding political power, and having a direct role in the making of legislative decisions, be contingent on their social status. Short of total direct democracy, which would be hard to administer in a country the size of the UK, random selection would seem to most strongly draw out the *democratic* principle of representative democracy.[55]

The instrumental benefits, or happy side effects, of adopting a system of random selection are multiple, some striking directly at the core of the political-class narrative outlined in Chapter 1. In his work, Guerrero identifies further benefits of random selection. The first is the epistemic benefit offered by greater cognitive diversity. Simply, if members of the political class were randomly selected and served time-limited terms in the decision-making body, the chances of them bringing diverse perspectives, heuristics, and experiences to the table would be high.[56] As noted in Chapter 3, available evidence suggests that such a development might have a wide range of benefits. Though I am sceptical as to the extent to which we should allow our arguments in favour of diversity to rely on these claims, in another sense such cognitive diversity would likely result in the political class being more responsive to the interests and wishes of the wider population. This would primarily be because a wider and deeper slice of that population would literally be present when decisions were being made. Critically, although this would still not result in everyone feeling represented all of the time, it would probably guard against instances of individuals feeling completely disenfranchised from formal politics in the medium to long term. This would mean that any feeling of exclusion would be temporary, and individuals who felt excluded would know that it was not the result of patterns of systematic inequalities of various kinds. Any exclusion would be arbitrary and, quite literally, random.

Other potential benefits relate to further elements of the political-class narrative. Many critics of the political class accuse its members of having an arrogant disdain for the public at large. Guerrero suggests that politicians selected randomly via lot would be unlikely to harbour such attitudes, their demeanour instead reflecting a 'humility of the chosen'. If one knows that holding a potentially powerful or prestigious position of decision-making is completely unrelated to any personal qualities or characteristics one might hold, the potential for being even slightly smug about the situation dissipates. The political-class narrative has also focused on the venal nature of that class, with a general thought that its members are in it for themselves and are feathering their own nests rather than being concerned about ours. Guerrero refers to this idea as 'capture': 'An elected official is captured if he or she uses his or her position to advance the interests of the powerful, rather than to create policy that is responsive or good (when doing so would conflict with the interests of the powerful).'[57] He notes that this kind of capture is more likely to occur when running for office is more difficult: the greater number of gatekeepers present, and the greater number of hurdles that need to be jumped (financial costs and other resource-draining activities, for example), the more likely it becomes that those with greater resources to dole out will effectively control who can run for office.[58] In many advanced democracies, elections (in the first instance and in the case of re-election) work something like this.[59] Although the veracity of these kinds of claims can be brought into question, the suspicion of capture having occurred might be stamped out altogether under a system of random selection by lot. As Guerrero notes, powerful interests would have no reason to encourage or aid the candidacies of certain individuals, would have no need (and therefore no ability) to help them get re-elected, and, given the likely frequent rotation of membership, any attempt at capture would be costly. Additionally, and perhaps more importantly, institutions would no longer be subject to capture by the parties themselves. If political parties are unrepresentative in the sense that very few people tend to get involved in them, for all kinds of reasons, then those who make it to their upper echelons and into political institutions are very unusual in comparison with the everyday citizen. Random selection would remove this requirement of intense political involvement with a chosen party.

A further related potential benefit of randomly selecting our politicians is that, no longer facing re-election on a five-yearly basis, they might display an increased willingness to take decisions on issues that offer politicians almost no electoral benefits if they deal with them. To return to the example in Chapter 3, climate change is an issue that undoubtedly will affect democracies old and new in the years, decades, and centuries to come, but it is unlikely to make politicians who address it popular. Conversely, it is almost certainly likely to make them unpopular, at least with some. Decisions on issues of this kind are arguably the most important of all. Economists have referred to them as 'intemporal choices', which see politicians at risk of displaying 'time preference', which is 'the preference for immediate utility over delayed utility'.[60] Without elections, the political class might be expected to better focus on the issue at hand and make decisions without regard for the future health of their own careers.

How Could We Randomly Select Representatives?

I do not wish to be too prescriptive about the specifics of any possible system based on the principle of random selection, as any details would be best decided in a democratic fashion. There are, however, instructional examples from across time and space that can give us an idea of how this system might function.

The key considerations would centre on the powers of the randomly selected body and the scope of its concerns. For example, a decision might need to be made regarding the relationship of the body to any existing elected legislatures, with the selected body either supplementing, overriding, or replacing these. In terms of scope, the selected body might act in the way that most national legislatures currently do and design legislation in all conceivable areas, or it may instead focus on a single issue or issue area. As I said, I do not wish to offer any definitive pronouncements here, but I do think it critical that any such body that came to exist should have real power, and not be simply advisory. Making a randomly selected body solely advisory in nature would be to miss the point of what I have laid out in previous chapters, and would effectively act to undermine it (the continued existence of a presumably truly powerful elected body acting as a knowledgeable parent watching over the randomly selected child who is assumed to be constantly on the verge of causing some kind of harm). An alternative somewhere between the two poles of solely advisory and all-powerful is something akin to the current House of Lords, which could become a sort of randomly selected senate.[61] This might have increased formal powers compared with the current Lords, but as has been discussed at length by parliamentary scholars, striking a workable balance of power between the two chambers would be difficult. Overall, though, introducing such an element might go some way to diluting the perception that *all* politicians were the same, and any introduction of random selection would increase the likelihood that the average citizen would either serve in the assembly herself or would know someone who had done so or currently did.

The question of scope is perhaps more interesting. Guerrero favours a system of single-issue assemblies focused on individual policy areas such as health, the environment, and industry. Once randomly selected from the eligible population, the assembly would take evidence from a series of experts and stakeholders in the issue area before entering a period of deliberation together. He proposes that 300 members would serve rotating terms (with a turnover of 100 members each year) and be paid 'considerable' amounts of money to serve, either a standardized sum or a multiplier of current salary.[62] More specifically, he writes that '[E]ach single-issue lottery-selected legislature (SILL) would meet for two legislative sessions each calendar year, and the structure for each session would be something like this: agenda setting, learning phase with expert presentations, community consultation, deliberation/discussion, drafting, revising, and voting'.[63]

Keith Sutherland outlines a detailed and comprehensive proposal for the use of random selection of political representation in his book *A People's Parliament*.[64] Sutherland's primary concern is with codifying the principle of executive–legislative separation in the British political system. His proposal combines a randomly selected assembly with an appointed executive and a further chamber of party-political advocates who help to bring issues to the table. The legislative chamber would also include a number of what Sutherland calls 'Lords Advocate', experts in various fields appointed to guide, inform, and raise awareness of issues amongst the randomly selected assembly members. However, the Lords Advocate are restricted to this hand-holding role and cannot themselves vote on legislative proposals. Executive appointments, made on the basis of perceived merit in a given field (e.g. health, education, and so on) are made by the monarch but must be approved by the randomly selected members.[65] Sutherland makes a few suggestions that those randomly selected members should meet some basic level of competence, with measures such as IQ or another metric being mooted. Overall, and despite best efforts, it seems to me that Sutherland's approach ultimately has to let back in many of the perceived evils it sets out to eradicate from British political life, most notably political parties. Moreover, the reliance on merit and the assumption that objective standards of expertise will exist outside of those areas where it makes itself obvious (the British Medical Association in the area of health, for example) are problematic. Sutherland's book was published prior to the popularization of Hong and Page's work in the social sciences, and therefore unknowingly violates a number of their assumptions around maximizing diversity; the hurdle of the IQ test, for example, would presumably limit diversity beyond the level that the Hong–Page theorems require.

Even if the underlying logic laid out in previous chapters is accepted, much thought would need to go into the process of adopting a system of random selection for a legislative assembly. There are a number of key issues that would require us to think well outside the parameters we are used to. For one, it is not clear how accountability would play a role in such a system. To an extent, the traditional need for accountability is designed out of the system by default, but this may not prove satisfactory to all, especially if executive leaders were not randomly selected; and there are other questions to address here around the issue of how collective interests would be formulated and enter the political agenda in the first instance. Although it could well turn out that a healthy civic society would see the emergence of coalitions united by given policy preferences pushing issues on to the political agenda, it seems more likely that political parties of a kind would be necessary. That said, even if they persisted in their role of aggregation, parties would no longer be in possession of an effective veto over any proposals that threaten either their own interests or the interests of those they represent.[66] Second, and just as problematic, is the possibility that individuals would need to be coerced into performing their duties if selected to serve in the assembly. As discussed above, one would hope that the development of cultural norms that favoured and valued such service would take care of this, but there would undoubtedly be exceptions to this that would need to be dealt with.

This is but one option for solving the larger diversity issue which is the unifying element of the political-class narrative. I think it is probably the solution that hits most firmly at the core of the problem as stated, though detailed and careful thought would need to be given to its various implications if it was ever looking like it might be adopted. I also suspect that we are unlikely to see this solution adopted wholesale in the UK any time soon. Despite this, it is interesting to work through how the underlying principle of random selection may indeed solve many of the supposed ills associated with the current political class.

Conclusion

This chapter has considered a number of possible methods that could be used to increase the diversity of the political class. These have ranged from less controversial or radical reforms, some of which are already in place, to those which are more of an acquired taste, including randomly selecting members of the legislative assembly. Crucially, your likely favoured option when it comes to reform is going to depend on your diagnosis of the problem. If you are convinced by the argument from justice, reforms addressing the presence of traditionally under-represented groups will be preferred. Should your preoccupation instead be with the potential instrumental benefits of high levels of cognitive diversity among the political class, random selection might better match your aims. A further point of note is that any reform is as much about endorsing a particular vision of what democratic politics should be as it is about achieving a given outcome. I hope that the above discussion has caused readers to reflect both on their own, often tacit, thoughts on this matter, as well as push them to consider how our current dominant forms of political engagement do the same. I consider this further in the concluding chapter.

Conclusion

There is a representative failure at the heart of the political class, with its current members lacking the diversity of all kinds seen in the population as a whole, rendering them distant from those on whose behalf they act. This is the result of various forces greater than any individual—social inequality, economic shifts, demographic changes—but that does not render it unimpeachable. I have discussed potential remedies and the positives and negatives that each carry with them. By this point, you have probably come to some kind of judgement regarding the questions I raised at the beginning of the book and the answers I have offered. In this chapter, I will summarize what I see as the key messages put forward so far, and offer a broader consideration of what might be at stake in this debate as a whole. I focus on the question of why political actors (namely political parties) might actually wish to make some of the changes I suggest and what those of us already intensely involved in formal politics can do so as to avoid what I call epistemic snobbery.

Four Lessons

The following offers a brief summary of what I see as the key takeaway points of the book as a whole. They are not so much policy recommendations as points of reflection that, once considered, reframe the question of the political class.

1. Democracy requires inclusion

Although the possession of formal equal rights to political participation is far from insignificant, the continuing existence of a representative democracy plagued by a chronic failure of representation should not be ignored, and the multiple barriers systematically excluding individuals from traditionally under-represented groups must be acknowledged. As the arguments made at the opening of Chapter 3 made clear, *who* the representatives in a representative democracy are matters.

2. What counts as useful political knowledge is less than clear

Existing research in political science and cognate disciplines, as well as popular discussion of the concept, defines political knowledge in a limited way, often measuring it in a way that rewards the rote memorization of various procedural facts and figures. Other research has taken findings generated using these measures to argue that many members of the electorate in democratic states are not fit to vote in elections to decide who should hold political office or to hold office themselves. On reflection, though, that the possession of such knowledge is an aid to *political* decision-making is unclear at best. Although it would certainly aid political actors involved in the process of passing laws whose content is already decided on, it is less clear that it would help in the more important step of deciding that same content. Deep down, these are always political judgements that cannot be adjudicated on definitively one way or the other, regardless of how much empirical evidence is generated about them.

3. Politics is, and always will be, uncertain

That politics is uncertain is a major premise of the book's argument, and it is one that I do not think is massively controversial. Although hindsight makes the path that events take seem clear and predictable, the lived reality is somewhat different. Although the world has undoubtedly become safer on a wide range of metrics, this has not made it more predictable or stable overall. New problems present themselves even in safe situations, and there is little chance that we will ever be in a situation without problems at all. As such, uncertainty is here to stay. As Hélène Landemore puts it:

Political problems . . . are unpredictable issues for which we cannot tell in advance who is going to have the relevant perspective. The rational attitude to have with respect to such questions is one of agnosticism as to who has the best answer to them, until that answer is tried in the public forum. The only thing we can tell about political problems is that solutions can come from anywhere and are unlikely to come always from the same people.[1]

4. Uncertainty may best be dealt with by diversity, not expertise

If we accept that uncertainty is here to stay, we need to consider how best to approach it. Many have argued that the optimal approach is to assemble a group of the best possible people for the job, a group of 'knowers', political experts, or experienced politicians. Such a group, the argument goes, will have an epistemic advantage over a wider group that may be more representative of the population as a whole but may also lack much of the experience and expertise purported to be relevant. Recent work by Lu Hong and Scott Page, discussed in Chapter 3, has brought this into question. Although I ultimately do not fully endorse this position, empirical evidence from existing real-world examples of citizen assemblies and other inclusive policy-making ventures also bring into question the idea that the average person simply is not capable of intensive political participation.

Based on the above, a number of suggestions as to how the diversification of the political class might be brought about were offered in the previous chapter. These included various equality-seeking strategies, such as the adoption of various electoral quotas, as well as the consideration of some element of random selection in the political system. As I made clear, I consider this a good answer to the problem of inequality's effects on the composition of the political class; but not the best answer. The optimal approach would be to eradicate at root the inequalities that result in such representative discrepancies. As this is unlikely to happen, certainly in any society that upholds a liberal commitment to institutions such as the family and private property, we should consider how to do our best to artificially limit the effects of such inequality. A further dose of pragmatism comes when we consider the question of why political actors would actually undertake any of these reforms.

Why Would Political Actors Seek Reform?

A response that I expect a number of people to have to this book is that, although they broadly agree with it as a whole, they do not see any real need to act on its suggestions, and do not understand why political actors, primarily political parties, would either. I sympathize, but only to a point.

We can theorize various possible incentives that parties might have to diversify their candidate pool and, consequently, the political class as a whole. For some, this will be seen as something of an ideological imperative. Traditionally, parties of the left have put in superior performances compared with their counterparts on the right when it comes to increasing the numbers of women and individuals from ethnic minorities on their parliamentary benches. This, it has been said, is thanks to the greater commitment to egalitarianism that is inherent in such left-wing political agendas. However, this clearly cannot be the only explanation, given the rate at which political parties on the right of the ideological spectrum have improved their own performance on these metrics in recent years.[2] Some have suggested that this is reflective of perceived (if not actual) electoral incentives offered to parties by voters who are keen to see more women and candidates from other traditionally under-represented groups in all parties. On this view, parties will be pushed to adopt reforms that promote diversity by the electoral equivalent of market forces—they will do it because it is good for them.

It is also plausible that the public mood might push parties of all stripes towards such a strategy. If it became apparent that the threat of even greater public withdrawal from the formal processes of politics was imminent, and that diversifying the candidate and representative pool might stem this flow, political actors across the board might act in something akin to a mode of self-preservation. Richard Dawkins's idea of the 'selfish gene' can be applied here. It is not that the gene is selfish in the sense that it is morally knowing, but rather that it will behave in an evolutionarily stable way that ensures that its genetic material is passed on by protecting itself against the insurgent strategies of other genes.[3] More often than not, such a strategy takes the form of altruism. In other words, it is programmed to survive. The political class as a whole may one day feel the same way and react accordingly.

Finally, one might hope that political parties, and the actors within them, will have some additional commitment to democratic principles that may prompt them to behave in the ways I have discussed. A strong normative commitment to democratic notions of inclusion and equality may prey on the minds of politicians unsatisfied with the way things currently are. I think we can find evidence that this is already the case in the actions of MPs who have sought to understand exactly why the public dislikes them so much. We might see the establishment and work of the House of Commons Political and Constitutional Reform Committee, led for some time by Graham Allen MP, in this light.[4] Crucially, change in the direction of greater political equality is only going to come about if those who currently benefit from the status quo, and who hold (or are likely to hold in future) positions of political and social power, are willing to relinquish them. As I have suggested, this means that politics will need to be seen as something other than an arena for the realization of individual ambitions for both politicians and the wider sphere of people who are currently intensely involved in formal politics.

What to Do?

One of my hopes for this book is that those who read it might, if they did not already do so, begin to consider the issue of the political class, and other criticisms of political elites, as issues of representation and equality, and as part of a bigger question about who is deemed eligible to participate in political life. In particular, I hope that it emboldens people to be critical on this final point, causing them to dispute commonly held ideas about who is entitled to be heard in political discussions, and what kinds of spurious qualifications are required to do so. On this question our political air is, in the words of Christopher Hitchens, 'thick with bullshit'.[5] If it does little else, I hope that this book will do its own small part to act as something of a thinning breeze. Any suggestion that a professionalized political class can be justified on the grounds that politics is now primarily a technocratic exercise in implementation, rather than an arena of ideological contestation, must be rejected. Such a suggestion would be misguided. For better or worse, the end point of politics is, and forever will be, more politics and more disagreement. Attractive as the alternative might seem, it is simply wrong.

In making this argument, I am not merely chasing shadows. In the wake of Brexit and the election of Donald Trump, a pernicious elitism can be seen to have asserted itself. In the seven days either side of the US election, both the *New York Times* and the *Guardian* ran opinion pieces espousing support for hereditary monarchy as a useful complement to electoral democracy.[6] Although these arguments are more than just faintly ludicrous, their encroachment into the political sphere should concern those of a democratic disposition. As I have argued in all that has preceded this conclusion, the simultaneously juvenile and faux-nostalgic pang that a lone monarch will be somehow superior to the people they rule over by virtue of birth is without any kind of basis. The same can be said of the leaders of many of the so-called 'populist' movements currently in the ascendancy in many democracies, most of which are led by individuals who are from firmly privileged socio-economic backgrounds.

Ultimately, the threat here is that our defences of democratic institutions themselves become anti-democratic. Although political scientists and other political figures may need to defend democratic institutions in various ways against the attacks these people mount, we should not allow this to act as total absolution of these institutions' ills, and nor should we conflate the statements of political plutocrats, termed 'populist' by the media, with what a genuine popular democracy might actually look like. Rather than being indicative of an actual popular movement, these parties and figures are more often than not based on familiar sources of wealth and societal power and involve an extremely small number of intensely politically involved individuals. They are categorically *not* large-scale popular movements, and their fledgling success should not be seen as akin to meeting the conditions of widespread political participation I have discussed in this book.

So, what can we as individuals do to change things? First, if you are someone who has previously assumed that you had nothing to contribute to, or lacked the qualifications to speak in, political discussions, I hope to have disabused you of this notion. In some way, everyone has something to say about politics, whether they realize it or not.

Second, and more interesting, is the question of what those of us who are currently involved in, or associated with, politics in an intense way should do. In this group, I would include elected officials at all levels, those who work professionally in politics, political journalists and commentators and, increasingly, political scientists. Recent years have seen a rise in the prominence and status of political scientists in both the media and political institutions, a result of the structural incentives offered by the Research Excellence Framework (REF) for activities that either disseminate research findings or bring about impact in policy or cultural terms. In principle this is a good thing. I have yet to meet an academic who is reluctant to discuss their work, and many are good at simplifying the complexities of what they do to make it accessible to a wider audience. This development is on the one hand clearly positive, allowing political science to offer the public and political actors new ways to consider political issues. On the other hand, it has made political scientists simultaneously more visible and powerful than they have ever previously been, firmly locating them as part of the professionalized political commentariat that both comments on, and makes, the political weather. In short, political scientists have become political actors and, although they may claim to be object-ive or non-partisan, they can never be considered non-political. In November 2016 Will Jennings and Martin Lodge, both senior political scientists based in the UK, wrote:

The role of the academic as pundit has increasingly pitched political scientists into the media limelight. While advancing public understanding of politics should unquestionably be a mission for the discipline, this creates pressure to hype findings, condense them into the confines of a tweet, or offer analysis to meet the demands of short-term news cycles rather than posing more critical questions about the nature of social and political change (or questioning the assumptions of our data and models), or even challenge the way in which pol-itics is done and the media package it. This pressures researchers to favour punditry (making bold predictions about outcomes and basking in applause for their foresight) above deeper diagnosis of long-term trends. It also often makes them inseparable from the politics they seek to analyse.[7]

The risk is that political scientists, along with other members of the intensely politically engaged, do not help to bridge the gap between the formal political world and those who are currently displaying little interest in it, but instead themselves assist in extending the barriers between the two.[8] Mischaracterizing politics as something that can be 'solved' factually, and putting oneself or one's discipline forward as an objective arbiter in this pursuit, is fraught with potential pitfalls. A dif-ferent approach would be more suitable, one that didn't paint political scientists as being expert in the answering of political questions (as opposed to the description and analysis of events or trends) or as some-how being able to participate in political discussions with total object-ivity. Further, increasing pressure on academics to coordinate with members of the media and political operatives is going to affect both how research, and the dissemination of that research, take place.

In this vein, it is too often the case that people's initial forays into politics are treated disparagingly by members of the media or the academic commentariat. The somewhat unexpected rise of Jeremy Corbyn, discussed earlier in the book, has seen epistemic elitists uncloak themselves in both of these groups. For example, Janan Ganesh, a columnist for the *Financial Times*, tweeted the following in August 2016: 'You can do analysis of Corbyn and his "movement" (I have done it) but the essence of the whole thing is that they are just thick as pigshit.'[9] Jonathan Dean, a political theorist, has also noted a similar tendency among academics to write off the democratic involvement that Corbyn appears to have inspired. Dean writes that political scientists have repeatedly failed to correct 'a number of factual inaccuracies about Corbyn supporters', have displayed 'disinterest and at times outright hostility' towards his success at increasing the size of Labour's membership, and that both of these behaviours are 'marked by a thinly concealed partisan opposition to Corbyn's politics'.[10] The point here is not that Corbyn's supporters are 'right' about the issues they campaign on, but rather that it is not healthy to simply dismiss them out of hand, largely on the basis of what appear to be ad hominem attacks. Arguably, consistently asserting the pointlessness of the new members' and supporters' endeavour displays a fundamental suspicion of political discourse that is not synonymous in form or content with recognized 'expert' sources. This kind of epistemic snobbery is only going to damage efforts to maintain democratic systems of government in the long run. Humility regarding our expertise, and self-reflection on our role, are called for.

What stance should we, both as individuals and as a group of more politically influential and powerful people, adopt when engaging with the wider public, most of whom lack such power and influence? The comedian Chris Rock, discussing the power relations that he has found himself navigating as a wealthy and successful stand-up comic who often ridicules others as part of his act, has stated that his watchword is to be 'always punching upwards'.[11] The idea here is that in a given domain, be it politics or comedy, it is wrong to proceed without acknowledging the massive differentials in power that are inherent in any interaction between the individual with the mouthpiece and everyone listening. In Rock's case, he does not feel it is right for him, as a multimillionaire celebrity, to 'punch down' on people beneath him in terms of wealth, fame, and so on. Although few political scientists are millionaires, many of us reside in the upper end of the income distribution.[12] We are highly educated, have strong social networks, and, as noted, hold an increasing amount of political influence. Consequently, it is my view that we need to be sure that we are not punching down. Although it might be professionally opportune to do so, and in turn to avoid punching up at the truly political powerful, we should avoid this temptation. Something like this principle should be the basis of a kind of ethics of engagement for the intensely politically involved. Practically, this means we should place the utterances of actually powerful individuals under far more scrutiny than we do to the political speech of the average citizen, and we should be cognizant of the ways in which we develop relationships with individuals possessing significant political power or influence. Those of us who are closer to politics than most of our fellow citizens should, to adopt Robert Goodin's phrase, avoid being 'handmaidens to power', something perhaps especially true of political commentators and political scientists.[13]

Following the 2008 financial crash, academics working in the discipline of economics have had to face up to their shortcomings in a similar way. In their 2016 book *The Econocracy*, Joe Earle, Cahal Moran, and Zach Ward-Perkins discuss how the crisis made it clear that the existing model for generating and conveying economic expertise to the general public had to change. In particular, they wanted to point out that, in public discussions of economics, 'there is an important role for experts... but this role is as a humble advisor not a detached authority figure'.[14] I think political scientists, students, and the wider network of individuals involved in formal political organizations are in a similar position. Earle and his colleagues define 'econocracy' as the idea that the economy is a 'distinct system with its own internal logic that requires experts to manage it'.[15] We can see traces of equivalent thinking within the political studies community. Again, Will Jennings and Martin Lodge take note of

the craze to create 'public policy schools' so as to inform global elites of students about policy experiences, global challenges and international networking. Such programmes have been attractive in financial terms to universities, they have proven to be a convenient vehicle to attract high profile donors, and they offer opportunities for students to mingle.... Critical questioning is unlikely to feature on such programmes given that learning outcomes are about enhancing 'rationality'.[16]

The Blavatnik School of Government at the University of Oxford, for example, states that its purpose is 'educating leaders. Simple as that'.[17] I do not doubt the sincerity of this approach but, focused as it is on training a small number of individuals to 'address some of this century's most complex public policy challenges', it is misguided. One worries that the institutional, financial, and cultural incentives to complicate these issues to the point where ever more experts are required, and more training needed, may prove too strong a barrier to actually solving them. Of course, a weaker version of this critique might also apply to a political-studies or political-science curriculum that increasingly pitches politics graduates as the future employees of politicians, think tanks, or political institutions, and as the political leaders of the future. There is a huge amount to be said in favour of studying politics at university, but I am unconvinced that making the possession of a degree in politics a prerequisite for intense political participation will do anything other than encourage epistemic snobbery and reduce political participation in the long run.

Such epistemic snobbery also serves to delegitimize the actions of regular citizens who have only recently entered into what is recognizably political activity, with the underlying assumption that one needs to have the 'correct' kinds of experience or expertise to be worth listening to in the course of political discussion. As I have argued, I think this is an untenable position. Broader societal inequalities result in all kinds of reasons that individuals might not have been able to build up such currency and, more than this, I do not think we should want politics to be filled with experienced old hands. At the risk of sounding glib, this approach hasn't exactly done us a power of good in recent years. In many ways, politicians, celebrities, the media, academics, and other intensely politically involved groups have shown themselves to be no match for the task of monopolizing public discussion on political issues.[18] It should not be the case that the only people who end up being sufficiently credentialed to comment on political matters are those who have been unusually interested in an extremely limited form of institutional politics from a young age. As David Estlund puts it:

There are certain people to whom the public often turns for expert political advice, such as pundits, politicians, political scientists, and so on. Such people are often consulted by journalists, and by extension, their readers. They publish books, articles, and columns that are treated with some deference by the public. How expert are they? Well, since there is no publicly agreed standard for scoring their political advice as correct or incorrect, we cannot, as a public, tell. It is not likely that they are, as a class, unusually accurate given that they disagree with each other apparently about as much as ordinary citizens do.[19]

I am not suggesting that expert-derived factual knowledge of various kinds should not bear on political discussions, as it should. But we need to acknowledge that political questions cannot be addressed solely through the accumulation of factual knowledge. This kind of knowledge gives us answers only in the context of wider value judgements. And, although we should consider this evidence when thinking through our views on matters of this kind, it can only bring us so far. To collectively address political questions, it is not the case that we simply need to assemble the 'most qualified' people and wait patiently for them to come up with the 'right answer'. It does not work like that now, and it never will.

So, all told, we should aim to include a more diverse range of people in our political life and, in doing so, reclaim it as a collective endeavour in which we all have a role to play. Only then, perhaps, will we be able to see politics as something that happens here with us and not there with them, and as something that we are all that much closer to.

Notes

INTRODUCTION

1. I appreciate that elections do give us a voice in a sense, but only as a collective entity and with the various manipulations and compromises that this brings.
2. See, for example, Gerry Stoker (2006), *Why Politics Matters*, Basingstoke: Palgrave Macmillan.
3. There is an enormous amount of evidence for this claim—see, for example, http://www.bbc.co.uk/news/uk-politics-29682077, and https://www.ipsos-mori.com/researchpublications/researcharchive/3504/Politicians-trusted-less-than-estate-agents-bankers-and-journalists.aspx. Historical data is harder to come by, but the available evidence suggests that trust in politicians has been in decline for some time now. The AntiPolitics project underway at the University of Southampton promises to tell us more about historic levels of trust in politics in the coming years, and a working paper is available at http://antipolitics.soton.ac.uk/files/2014/10/egc-working-paper-2015.pdf.
4. Peter Mair (2013), *Ruling the Void: The Hollowing of Western Democracy*, London: Verso.
5. Matthew Goodwin and Caitlin Milazzo (2015), *UKIP*, Oxford: Oxford University Press, Kindle pp. 341–54.
6. Uwe Jun (2003), 'Great Britain: From the Prevalence of the Amateur to the Dominance of the Professional Politician' in *The Political Class in Advanced Democracies*, ed. Jens Borchert and Jurgen Zeiss, Oxford: Oxford University Press, pp. 164–86; Paul Cairney (2007), 'The Professionalisation of MPs: Refining the "Politics-Facilitating" Explanation', *Parliamentary Affairs* 60(2): pp. 212–33; Peter Allen (2013), 'Linking the pre-parliamentary political experience and political careers of the 1997 General Election cohort', *Parliamentary Affairs* 66(4): pp. 685–70; Peter Allen and Paul Cairney (2015), 'What do we mean when we talk about the "political class"?', *Political Studies Review*, advance online access.
7. Readers can find a concise but detailed introduction to these ideas in Colin Hay (2002), *Political Analysis: A Critical Introduction*, Basingstoke: Palgrave Macmillan.
8. Distressing as such a simple definition might prove for some readers, I do not want to become fixated on varying interpretations at this point. There is further discussion of this issue at the beginning of Chapter 3.

9. Nadia Urbinati (2006), *Representative Democracy: Principles & Genealogy*, Chicago: Chicago University Press.

10. Urbinati (2006), pp. 6–7.

11. Urbinati (2006), p. 10.

12. David Plotke (1997), 'Representation is Democracy', *Constellations* 4(1), pp. 19–34: p. 19.

13. The relationship between descriptive and substantive representation has been the cause of much spilled ink in political science, especially in the gender and politics literature. The question has generally been whether increased numbers of women result in a better substantive representation of women's interests. Readers might share the scepticism of many theorists regarding the notion of 'interests'. Even if these could be defined, as the political scientist Sarah Childs has astutely noted, a woman's body does not a feminist mind make.

14. Jeffrey Edward Green (2016), *The Shadow of Unfairness: A Plebeian Theory of Liberal Democracy*, New York: Oxford University Press, p. 36.

15. This definition draws on Iris Marion Young's (2000) definition in *Inclusion and Democracy*, Oxford: Oxford University Press, p. 6.

16. The philosopher Miranda Fricker offers a full treatment of the idea of epistemic injustice in her (2007) book *Epistemic Injustice: Power & the Ethics of Knowing*, Oxford: Oxford University Press. I don't engage with her framework in this book, but readers interested in this idea might wish to seek it out elsewhere.

17. One issue with advocating this approach is that it is never abundantly clear how hard and fast the boundaries of identities actually are, making it difficult to adjudicate when an infringement has occurred.

18. Thomas Piketty (2014), *Capital in the Twenty-First Century*, trans. Arthur Goldhammer, Cambridge, MA: Harvard University Press.

19. See a November 2015 report from the Institute for Fiscal Studies on this subject for more: http://www.ifs.org.uk/publications/8050.

20. http://www.theguardian.com/politics/2015/may/06/number-of-mps-who-earn-from-renting-out-property-rises-by-a-third.

21. Peter Mair (2013) presents a wide range of evidence in favour of this contention in his *Ruling the Void: The Hollowing of Western Democracy*, London: Verso.

22. Oliver Heath (2015), 'Policy Representation, Social Representation and Class Voting in Britain', *British Journal of Political Science* 45(1): pp. 173–93.

23. Jeffrey Edward Green (2015), 'Liberalism and the Problem of Plutocracy', *Constellations* 23(1): pp. 84–95.

24. There are multiple examples of this. The government has discussed removing housing benefit entitlement from adults under the age of 25. Similarly, the Educational Maintenance Allowance, provided to students from low-income families in post-16 school education, has been scrapped. On top of this, the government is moving to remove any grant provision for university students from low-income backgrounds, replacing these with loans.

25. Geoff Evans and James Tilley (2015), 'The new class war: Excluding the working class in 21st-century Britain', *Juncture* 21(4): pp. 298–304.

26. http://chronicle.com/article/Scholars-Talk-Writing-Steven/237315.

CHAPTER I

1. Michael Kenny (2009), 'Taking the Temperature of the Political Elite 2: The Professionals Move In?', *Parliamentary Affairs* 62(2), pp. 335–49: p. 337.

2. Thanks to Paul Cairney for his discussion on many of the points raised in this chapter. Together we have published an article titled 'What do we mean when we talk about the "political class"?', which takes a more academic view of the matter and might be of interest to keen readers.

3. Gaetano Mosca (1960), *The Ruling Class*, trans. Hannah D. Kahn, New York: McGraw-Hill.

4. Uwe Jun (2003), 'Great Britain: From the Prevalence of the Amateur to the Dominance of the Professional Politician', in *The Political Class in Advanced Democracies*, ed. Jens Borchert and Jürgen Zeiss, Oxford: Oxford University Press, pp. 164–86.

5. Owen Jones (2014), *The Establishment: And how they get away with it*, London: Allen Lane.

6. Jones (2014), p. 2.

7. Jeffrey Edward Green (2016), *The Shadow of Unfairness: A Plebeian Theory of Liberal Democracy*, New York: Oxford University Press.

8. I think this would also depend on political context. In the United States, for example, I can see that senior state-level legislators could easily be included in such a definition owing to their power. Indeed, in the UK, the mayor of London might similarly be considered a powerful enough figure to warrant inclusion.

9. I appreciate that devolution has made a dent in this power, but I do not think it is enough of a dent to have affected the core tenets of the long-standing 'Westminster Model'. See, for example, David Marsh (2008), 'Understanding British Government: Analysing Competing Models', *Parliamentary Affairs* 10(2): pp. 251–68.

10. In this sense, I generally discuss the UK case *exempli gratia*. Though some of the specifics in the narrative are probably unique to the UK, the underlying principles of the narrative, and the argument I make in the book, probably have application in most advanced Western democracies.

11. There is a substantial body of academic work that examines the socio-demographic backgrounds of MPs: Michael Rush (1969), *The Selection of Parliamentary Candidates*, London: Thomas Nelson & Sons; Colin Mellors (1978), *The British MP: A socio-economic study of the House of Commons*, Farnborough: Saxon House; Anthony King (1983), 'The Rise of the Career Politician in Britain – And Its Consequences', *British Journal of Political Science* 11(3): pp. 249–85; Dennis Kavanagh (1992), 'Changes in the Political Class and its Culture', *Parliamentary Affairs* 45(1): pp. 18–32; Michael Rush

(1994), 'Career Patterns in British Politics: First Choose Your Party...', *Parliamentary Affairs* 47(4): pp. 566–82; Pippa Norris and Joni Lovenduski (1995), *Political Recruitment: Gender, Race and Class in the British Parliament*, Cambridge: Cambridge University Press; Heinrich Best, Valerie Cromwell, Christopher Hausmann, and Michael Rush (2001), 'The Transformation of Legislative Elites: The Cases of Britain and Germany since the 1860s', *The Journal of Legislative Studies* 7(3): pp. 65–91; Paul Cairney (2007), 'The Professionalisation of MPs: Refining the "Politics-Facilitating" Explanation', *Parliamentary Affairs* 60(2): pp. 212–33.

12. Oxbridge is a portmanteau word for Oxford and Cambridge universities.

13. This was aided by the growth of party machinery surrounding elections and the rise of the 'permanent campaign' (see Catherine Needham (2005), 'Brand Leaders: Clinton, Blair and the Limitations of the Permanent Campaign, *Political Studies* 53(2): pp. 343–61 and Paul Herrnson (1994), 'Congress's Other Farm Team: Congressional Staff', *Polity* 27(1): pp. 137–56).

14. Best et al. (2001), p. 80.

15. https://www.theguardian.com/theguardian/2013/aug/09/andy-burnham-interview-thinking-bigger.

16. Pre-1987 data from Feargal McGuinness (2010), *Social Background of MPs*, House of Commons Library Research Note SN/SG/1528, Westminster: House of Commons.

17. The 'politician/political organizer' [sic] category is somewhat amorphous and in some ways is quite an odd categorization. As I have written about elsewhere (see Peter Allen (2013), 'Linking the pre-parliamentary political experience and political careers of the 1997 General Election cohort', *Parliamentary Affairs* 66(4): pp. 685–707), this category would not seem to include local councillors but only 'politicians' in the sense of former MPs or, following the late 1990s, Members of the Scottish Parliament (MSPs) or Members of the Welsh Assembly (AMs). However, the arguably more interesting category would be political organizers, loosely defined, on their own. In my other work I have claimed that there are probably better classifications of pre-parliamentary experience, especially *political* experience, that we could adopt. My favoured distinction is between national and local pre-parliamentary political experience, as this seems to tap into the more interesting tensions at play in many of these debates. Given the constraints of existing data, however, I stick here to the long-standing terminology used by Byron Criddle in his sections of the various *The British General Election* series. See Byron Criddle (1987), 'MPs and Candidates', in *The British General Election of 1987*, ed. David Butler and Dennis Kavanagh, New York: St. Martin's Press, pp. 191–210; Byron Criddle (1992), 'MPs and Candidates', in *The British General Election of 1992*, ed. David Butler and Dennis Kavanagh, Basingstoke: Palgrave Macmillan, pp. 211–30; Byron Criddle (1997), 'MPs and Candidates', in *The British General Election of 1997*, ed. David Butler and Dennis Kavanagh, Basingstoke: Palgrave Macmillan, pp. 186–209; Byron Criddle (2001), 'MPs and Candidates', in *The British General Election of 2001*,

ed. David Butler and Dennis Kavanagh, Basingstoke: Palgrave Macmillan, pp. 182–207; Byron Criddle (2005), 'MPs and Candidates', in *The British General Election of 2005*, ed. Dennis Kavanagh and David Butler, Basingstoke: Palgrave Macmillan, pp. 146–67; Byron Criddle (2010), 'More Diverse Yet More Uniform: MPs and Candidates', in *The British General Election of 2010*, ed. Dennis Kavanagh and Philip Cowley, Basingstoke: Palgrave Macmillan, pp. 306–29; Byron Criddle (2015), 'Variable Diversity: MPs and Candidates', in *The British General Election of 2015*, ed. Philip Cowley and Dennis Kavanagh, Basingstoke: Palgrave Macmillan, pp. 336–60.

18. I am not including full-time trade union representatives in this category; they are classified as miscellaneous.

19. Allen (2013).

20. http://www.parliament.uk/about/how/guides/factsheets/members-elections/m04/.

21. http://www.ons.gov.uk/peoplepopulationandcommunity/culturalidentity/ethnicity/articles/ethnicityandnationalidentityinenglandandwales/2012-12-11; https://policyexchange.org.uk/publication/a-portrait-of-modern-britain/.

22. http://www.bbc.co.uk/news/uk-politics-22309268.

23. http://www.bbc.co.uk/news/uk-politics-17815769.

24. For example, Ivor Jennings writes about the 'bright young men' who want to 'go into politics' but 'have no money' and have to be 'advised accordingly' (Ivor Jennings (1957), *Parliament*, Cambridge: Cambridge University Press, p. 58).

25. https://www.theguardian.com/housing-network/2016/jan/14/mp-landlords-number-risen-quarter-last-parliament-housing-bill.

26. https://www.theatlantic.com/politics/archive/2014/09/how-did-members-of-congress-get-so-wealthy/379848/.

27. http://www.suttontrust.com/wp-content/uploads/2015/05/Parliamentary-Privilege-The-MPs-2015-2.pdf.

28. http://webarchive.nationalarchives.gov.uk/20160105160709/http://www.ons.gov.uk/ons/dcp171776_337841.pdf.

29. http://www.spectator.co.uk/2014/09/the-politics-of-ppe/.

30. https://www.theguardian.com/tv-and-radio/video/2015/dec/18/david-dimbleby-eton-tory-mp-jacob-rees-mogg-video.

31. http://www.suttontrust.com/wp-content/uploads/2015/05/Parliamentary-Privilege-The-MPs-2015-2.pdf.

32. King (1983).

33. http://webarchive.nationalarchives.gov.uk/20160105160709/http://www.ons.gov.uk/ons/rel/pop-estimate/population-estimates-for-uk–england-and-wales–scotland-and-northern-ireland/mid-2014/sty-ageing-of-the-uk-population.html.

34. Allen (2013), p. 702.

35. In this section and the next I distinguish broadly between attitudes and behaviour. I appreciate that, for some, this might be a difficult distinction to make cleanly, as in some cases the only way we can ascertain someone's

attitudes is by inferring them from their behaviour. I accept this, but for the purposes of this chapter and for maintaining the sanity of less philosophically inclined readers, I will keep them at least somewhat separate.

36. Peter Oborne (2008), *The Triumph of the Political Class*, London: Pocket Books.
37. Jones (2014).
38. Peter Oborne (2007, pp. 49–50) disagrees and highlights a number of instances of what he sees as the disdain of the political class for the rule of law.
39. Jones (2014), p. 6.
40. Jones (2014), p. 6.
41. Colin Hay (2007), *Why We Hate Politics*, Cambridge: Polity.
42. Goodwin and Milazzo (2015), p. 43.
43. Will Jennings and Gerry Stoker (2016), 'The Bifurcation of Politics: Two Englands', *The Political Quarterly*, 87(3): pp. 372–82.
44. Jennings and Stoker (2016), p. 381.
45. http://ukandeu.ac.uk/why-britain-backed-brexit%E2%80%8F/.
46. Oborne (2007), p. 5.
47. http://www.bbc.co.uk/news/uk-politics-eu-referendum-35616946.
48. http://blogs.spectator.co.uk/2016/02/eu-referendum-a-third-of-mps-could-still-back-brexit/.
49. Mair (2013). Thanks to one of the anonymous reviewers for this observation and phrasing.
50. Oborne (2007), p. xvii.
51. Oborne (2007), p. 3.
52. Oborne (2007), p. 6.
53. Oborne (2007), p. 63.
54. http://www.telegraph.co.uk/news/2016/06/22/remains-project-sneer-has-laid-bare-the-contempt-politicians-hav/.
55. http://www.theguardian.com/politics/2015/may/20/metropolitan-elite-britains-new-pariah-class.
56. http://www.telegraph.co.uk/news/2016/06/22/remains-project-sneer-has-laid-bare-the-contempt-politicians-hav/.
57. http://www.spiked-online.com/newsite/article/after-the-vote-the-implosion-of-the-political-class-eu-referendum-brexit/#.V442eZMrLow.
58. Kenny (2009), p. 337.
59. Rosie Campbell, Philip Cowley, Nick Vivyan, and Markus Wagner (2016), 'Legislator Dissent as a Valence Signal', *British Journal of Political Science*, First View, https://www.cambridge.org/core/journals/british-journal-of-political-science/article/legislator-dissent-as-a-valence-signal/C30ABAA6B88288337BA7C196B18D7CA9.
60. Campbell et al. (2016), p. 2.
61. Oborne (2007), p. xvi.
62. https://www.theguardian.com/commentisfree/2015/dec/14/british-party-democracy-long-slow-death-elites-cults.

63. https://www.theguardian.com/commentisfree/2015/oct/25/remembrance-day-for-people-not-politicians.
64. http://www.dailymail.co.uk/news/article-3028532/I-won-t-try-hide-fact-posh-says-Cameron-eating-hotdog-KNIFE-FORK.html.
65. http://www.express.co.uk/comment/columnists/leo-mckinstry/483342/Leo-McKinstry-on-Britain-s-political-class.
66. Andrew C. Eggers and Jens Hainmueller (2009), 'MPs for Sale? Returns to Office in Postwar British Politics', *British Journal of Political Science*, 103(4): pp. 513–33.
67. Sandra González-Bailon, Will Jennings, and Martin Lodge (2013), 'Politics in the Boardroom: Corporate Pay, Networks and the Recruitment of Former Parliamentarians, Ministers and Civil Servants in Britain', *Political Studies* 61(4): pp. 850–73.
68. González-Bailon et al. (2013), p. 869.
69. Judith Bara (2005), 'A Question of Trust: Implementing Party Manifestos', *Parliamentary Affairs* 58(3): pp. 585–99.
70. http://www.spectator.co.uk/2016/06/an-age-of-broken-promises/.
71. Oborne (2007), p. 242.
72. Moloney (2000), p. 125. Kevin Moloney (2000), 'The rise and fall of spin: Changes of fashion in the presentation of UK politics', *Journal of Public Affairs*, 1(2): pp. 124–35.
73. Leighton Andrews (2006), 'Spin: from tactic to tabloid', *Journal of Public Affairs*, 6: pp. 31–45.
74. http://www.auditofpoliticalengagement.org/assets/media/reports/Audit-of-Political-Engagement-13-2016.pdf.
75. Joni Lovenduski (2012), 'Prime Minister's questions as political ritual', *British Politics* 7(4): pp. 314–40.
76. http://www.newstatesman.com/uk-politics/2010/07/lib-dem-coalition-policies.

CHAPTER 2

1. For the sake of summer being related to warmth, let us assume that this fictional example is not set in the UK.
2. Max Weber (1919), *Politics as a Vocation*, available online at http://anthropos-lab.net/wp/wp-content/uploads/2011/12/Weber-Politics-as-a-Vocation.pdf.
3. That is not to say that all of these reasons will be benevolent, or unrelated to the health of their personal finances once they no longer hold office, but rather that they most likely do not seek election to office solely for the official salary that is offered. Timothy Besley (2004) offers a useful discussion of these issues in 'Paying Politicians: Theory and Evidence', *Journal of the European Economic Association*, 2 (2–3): pp. 193–215.

4. Phillip Norton (1994), 'The Growth of the Constituency Role of the MP', *Parliamentary Affairs* 47(4): pp. 705–20. See also Norton's reflections on constituency service in the wake of the murder of Labour MP Jo Cox in the summer of 2016: https://nortonview.wordpress.com/2016/06/22/mps-and-constituency-service/. Also, Nigel Jackson and Darren Lilleker (2011), 'Microblogging, Constituency Service and Impression Management: UK MPs and the Use of Twitter', *Journal of Legislative Studies* 17(1): pp. 86–105.

5. There are, of course, exceptions to this rule. Boris Johnson, for example, has shown himself to be remarkably adept at maintaining external employment while serving in the Commons.

6. I fear that this sentence is ripe for being taken out of context; to reiterate what I said at the outset of the chapter, I do not subscribe to this view, but it is worth reflecting on all the same.

7. Notable examples of this include Tony Benn and Margaret Thatcher in the UK, and Ted Kennedy in the US.

8. Suzanne Dovi (2007), *The Good Representative*, Malden, MA: Wiley-Blackwell, p. 2.

9. Dovi (2007), p. 10.

10. Matthew Flinders (2012), *Defending Politics*, Oxford: Oxford University Press, p. 145. My account of the effect that the media has on narratives around the political class is necessarily simplistic. Empirically establishing media effects is notoriously difficult and will surely become more so given the rise and proliferation of social media. However, not being able to causally establish a relationship does not mean it is non-existent. The media may be more or less important than they once were, or equally important in different ways. Either way, they contribute to the context in which politics and the political class exist. See Joseph N. Cappella and Kathleen Hall Jamieson (1996), 'News Frames, Political Cynicism, and Media Cynicism', *The Annals of the American Academy of Political and Social Science* 546(July): pp. 71–84, for evidence of the dual effects of negative political coverage on perceptions of both politicians and the media themselves.

11. Although it is worth noting that they themselves are often the source of these kinds of stories.

12. While I was writing this chapter, the challenge to Jeremy Corbyn's leadership of the Labour Party was ongoing and threw up a typical example of how this kind of story goes. Paul Waugh, the Executive Editor for Politics at the *Huffington Post*, tweeted: 'Even Barry Gardiner nodding along at front in shad cab to Neil Kinnock speech saying JC should stand down.' Within three minutes, Barry Gardiner responded with a tweet of his own: 'Sorry @paulwaugh you are not in the room and your information is wrong.' The exchange can be found at https://twitter.com/BarryGardiner/status/750025621732990977.

13. This is not to say that politicians, or any individuals holding positions of societal power, should simply be let off the hook, but rather that more thought should be given to the manner and content of reporting that purports to hold them to account.

14. http://news.bbc.co.uk/1/hi/uk_politics/6744581.stm.

15. Peter Mair (2006), 'Ruling The Void? The Hollowing of Western Democracy', *New Left Review* 42, pp. 25–51: p. 44.

16. Patrick Seyd and Paul Whiteley (2002), *High-Intensity Participation,* Ann Arbor, MI: University of Michigan Press.

17. Mair (2013), p. 78.

18. Mair (2013), p. 81. This guarantee is premised on the existence of a unified party platform representing the interests of those united under it. I return to the thorny issue of interest in Chapter 3.

19. Mair (2013), p. 82.

20. Mair (2013), pp. 84–5.

21. Flinders (2012), p. 143.

22. Mike Savage, Niall Cunningham, Fiona Devine, Sam Friedman, Daniel Laurison, Lisa McKenzie, Andrew Miles, Helene Snee, and Paul Wakeling (2015), *Social Class in the 21st Century*, London: Penguin Books.

23. Savage et al. (2015), chapter 10.

24. John Harris, columnist for the *Guardian*, writes of the crisis facing the contemporary Labour Party: 'As with the centre-left parties across Europe in the same predicament, Labour is a 20th-century party adrift in a new reality. Its social foundations – the unions, heavy industry, the nonconformist church, a deference to the big state that has long evaporated – are either in deep retreat or have vanished completely. Its name embodies an attachment to the supposed glories of work that no longer chimes with insecure employment and insurgent automation.' https://www.theguardian.com/commentisfree/2016/jun/29/whoever-leader-is-labour-may-never-recover-crisis.

25. Geoff Evans and James Tilley (2015), 'The New Class War: Excluding the Working Class in 21st-century Britain', *Juncture*, 21(4): pp. 298–304.

26. Evans and Tilley (2015), p. 303.

27. Mair (2013) offers an international summary, as do Stoker (2007) and Hay (2006).

28. Mair (2006), pp. 33–4.

29. This should not be taken as passing judgement on this kind of participation. There are many reasons why people might not have the time, inclination, or resources for further engagement with parties. I discuss some of these in Chapter 4. It is surely better to have more people involved, regardless of the intensity of their involvement, than not.

30. Mair (2006), p. 43.

31. In the next chapter I offer a normative case against this kind of criterion on the grounds of desirability and utility. However, another objection

would take issue with the selection mechanism it assumes to exist—that of election. In Chapter 4 I discuss the possibility of British democracy without elections. I do not outline this objection specifically at any point, but it is worth noting.

32. Rainbow Murray (2015), 'What makes a good politician? Reassessing the criteria used for political recruitment', *Politics & Gender* 11(4): pp. 770–6.

33. Murray (2015), p. 773.

34. See, for example, Rosie Campbell and Philip Cowley (2013), 'What Voters Want: Reactions to Candidate Characteristics in a Survey Experiment', *Political Studies* 62(4): pp. 745–65.

35. See, for example, Mair (2013), Hay (2007), and Stoker (2006).

36. Mark Blyth (2013), *Austerity: The History of a Dangerous Idea*, Oxford: Oxford University Press.

37. Hay (2007), p. 80.

38. Hay (2007), p. 83.

39. Hay (2007), p. 112.

40. Hay (2007), p. 83.

41. Andrew Gamble (2000), *Politics and Fate*, Cambridge: Polity, p. 2.

42. Hay (2007), p. 86.

43. http://www.newstatesman.com/politics/uk/2016/11/tony-blair-s-unfinished-business.

44. It is possible that diversity might be needed to legitimate the decision-making body in the eyes of those living under its authority. However, it strikes me that surely part of the legitimacy-generating value of this would be the existence of some sort of debate. As such, without any debate it is unlikely that much legitimacy would be generated regardless of who was present in the decision-making body. Instead, it would appear to us something like the way that assemblies such as the North Korean Assembly appear, as empty vessels.

45. A book in a similar vein to these, but which I do not discuss, is Ilya Somin (2012), *Democracy and Political Ignorance: Why Smaller Government is Smarter*, Redwood City, CA: Stanford University Press.

46. This classification is used by Hélène Landemore in her *Democratic Reason* (2012).

47. Philip Cowley (2014), 'Descriptive Representation and Political Trust: A Quasi-Experiment Utilising Ignorance', *Journal of Legislative Studies* 20(4): pp. 573–87.

48. Patrick Sturgis and Patten Smith (2010), 'Fictitious Attitudes Revisited: Political Interest, Knowledge and the Generation of Nonattitudes', *Political Studies* 58(1): pp. 66–84.

49. https://www.ipsos-mori.com/researchpublications/researcharchive/3188/Perceptions-are not-reality-the-top-10-we-get-wrong.aspx.

50. His study focuses on the US, but the available evidence from the UK suggests that we might expect to see similar patterns to those he identifies.

51. Scott Althaus (2002), *Collective Preferences in Democratic Politics: Opinion Surveys and the Will of the People*, New York: Cambridge University Press, p. 15.
52. Althaus (2002), pp. 14–16.
53. Althaus (2002), p. 17.
54. Althaus (2002), p. 20.
55. Althaus (2002, pp. 23–4) goes on to simulate public opinion if these kinds of informational asymmetries did not exist and finds that public opinion would be changed in important ways. Althaus notes that, 'After controlling for information effects, collective opinion tends to become less approving of presidents and Congress, more dovish and interventionist on foreign policy, less conservative on social, environmental, and equal rights issues, and more conservative on morality issues and questions about the proper limits of government activity,'
56. Bryan Caplan (2007), *The Myth of the Rational Voter*, Princeton, NJ: Princeton University Press, p. 10.
57. Caplan (2007), p. 206.
58. Jason Brennan (2011), *The Ethics of Voting*, Princeton, NJ: Princeton University Press.
59. Brennan (2011), p.1. Thanks to one of the anonymous reviewers of the manuscript of this book who pointed out that, although academics and journalists regularly exercise themselves with the fear of the tyranny of the majority, it is almost always the case that the tyrants are the minority exploiting everyone else.
60. Jason Brennan (2016), *Against Democracy*, Princeton, NJ: Princeton University Press.
61. Brennan distinguishes the rights to formal political participation such as voting or holding political office from broader civil liberties like freedom of speech or of association, claiming that his desire for restricting their usage by the unqualified only applies to the former owing to the potential to either acquire or exercise power over others that is inherent within them (2016, p.10). This seems like something of a stretch given the clear parallels, at least in terms of this kind of power, held by those who own media conglomerates, multinational corporations, and so on. Of course it is true that the state has powers of enforcement through coercion which these bodies do not have, but the line is certainly fuzzier than Brennan seems to assume.
62. Brennan (2016), p. 17. I return to this idea later on. Brennan essentially argues that this is a non-arbitrary form of political inequality but, as I argue in Chapter 3, it is an almost total reflection of entirely arbitrary societal inequalities. As such, I do not think the underlying premise holds.
63. Luciana Berger (2011), in an interview with Women's Parliamentary Radio, www.wpradio.co.uk.
64. Scott Althaus (2002), p. 19, links the two: 'Simple bits of factual information about the parties and players in politics, the rules of the political

game, and the issue positions taken by various actors help to orient people in the world of politics. They are also crucial in helping people arrive at opinions that conform to their political predispositions and are internally consistent with other opinions.'

CHAPTER 3

1. Robert A. Dahl (2003), 'Democratic Polities in Advanced Countries: Success and Challenge', paper presented at the Third Latin American and Caribbean Conference on Social Sciences. Available online at http:// bibliotecavirtual.clacso.org.ar/ar/libros/hegeing/Dahl.pdf.
2. For a lengthier exposition of this argument, see Thomas Christiano (2008), *The Constitution of Equality: Democratic Authority and its Limits*, New York: Oxford University Press, ch. 1.
3. Dahl (2003), p. 54.
4. Anne Phillips (1995), *The Politics of Presence*, Oxford: Oxford University Press.
5. Phillips (1995), p. 1.
6. This isn't to say that accountability simply disappears when we begin to think about presence. Phillips is not too specific on how the two interrelate, seeming to maintain that accountability can really only be considered in terms of 'ideas' (i.e. policy programmes).
7. Phillips (1995), p. 65. In addition to what Phillips terms 'discrimination', I would broaden this definition to include structural inequalities within society that hinder political participation in any way.
8. My argument here is similar to that of Stephen Coleman (2013), when he discusses narratives surrounding voting in elections in his book *How Voters Feel*, Cambridge: Cambridge University Press.
9. Gabriela Catterberg and Alejandro Moreno (2006), 'The Individual Bases of Political Trust: Trends in New and Established Democracies', *International Journal of Public Opinion Research*, 18(1): pp. 31–48.
10. Anne Phillips (2012), 'Representation and Inclusion', *Politics & Gender* 8(4): pp. 512–18.
11. Jane Mansbridge (1999), 'Should Blacks Represent Blacks and Women Represent Women? A Contingent "Yes"', *Journal of Politics* 61(3): pp. 628–57. Mansbridge has recently written about whether her arguments on sex and race apply in the case of the working class. She concludes that they do, but not to the same extent. She does, however, maintain that the descriptive representation of the working class matters for the representation of their interests. See Jane Mansbridge (2015), 'Should Workers Represent Workers?', *Swiss Political Science Review*, 21(2): pp. 261–70. Of course, as an anonymous reviewer of the manuscript of this book noted, workers cannot represent workers, by definition, but former workers can.
12. There is evidence for this claim, mainly in the form of research by Amy Alexander. Studying longitudinal data from twenty-five countries, she finds

that, 'An increase in the percentage of women in parliament contributes to an increase in women's beliefs in women's ability to govern. Ultimately, the analyses show that the most accurate portrayal of the relationship between women's presence in parliament and women's beliefs in women's ability to govern is a virtuous cycle of mutually reinforcing changes in women's empowerment as political leaders.' See Amy Alexander (2012), 'Change in Women's Descriptive Representation and the Belief in Women's Ability to Govern: A Virtuous Cycle', *Politics & Gender* 8, pp. 437–64: p. 438.

13. For a summary of existing empirical evidence to this effect, and the presentation of further original findings, see Sofie Marien and Marc Hooghe (2011), 'Does political trust matter? An empirical investigation into the relation between political trust and support for law compliance', *European Journal of Political Research* 50(2): pp. 267–91.

14. David Runciman (2013) discusses these issues in his book *The Confidence Trap*, Princeton, NJ: Princeton University Press, as does Matthew Flinders (2012) in *Defending Politics*, Oxford: Oxford University Press.

15. http://www.newstatesman.com/politics/2013/10/russell-brand-on-revolution. For the uninitiated, Old Spice is a brand of male grooming products that was extremely popular in the late twentieth century.

16. Russell Brand (2014), *Revolution*, London: Random House, p. 319.

17. http://www.telegraph.co.uk/news/uknews/law-and-order/8630533/Riots-the-underclass-lashes-out.html.

18. http://www.theguardian.com/uk/2011/aug/10/uk-riots-political-classes.

19. For now, I park the question of what 'better running' might actually mean. In this case, as with all that rely on the epistemic benefits of a more diverse group of politicians, it is necessary to have some sort of baseline assumption that we can at least designate certain political outcomes as 'better' or 'worse' than others. I am not on board with such an assumption and discuss a critique of it later in the chapter.

20. This research is spearheaded by Nicholas Carnes. Carnes's (2013) book *White Collar Government,* Chicago, IL: Chicago University Press, showcases his key findings. Jacob S. Hacker and Paul Pierson (2011), *Winner-Take-All Politics*, New York, NY: Simon & Schuster, is on a similar theme.

21. For a full discussion of Cole's ideas, see Anthony H. Birch (1979), *Representative and Responsible Government*, London: George Allen & Unwin.

22. Dirk Antonczyk, Bernd Fitzenberger, and Katrin Sommerfeld (2010), 'Rising Wage Inequality, the Decline of Collective Bargaining, and the Gender Wage Gap, *Labour Economics* 17(5): pp. 835–47.

23. Milton Lodge and Charles Taber (2013), *The Rationalizing Voter*, New York: Cambridge University Press.

24. Or indeed to any other characteristic, other than their 'merit' for the role.

25. It is also likely a proxy for arguments relating to social class. Again, see Mansbridge (2015), mentioned in note 12 of this chapter.

26. Samuel Beer (1982), *Modern British Politics*, London: Faber & Faber.

27. http://www.telegraph.co.uk/comment/telegraph-view/3561871/Politics-needs-real-people.html.

28. The philosopher L. A. Paul (2014) has written about this idea. She refers to these kinds of experiences, where you need to undergo the experience to understand what it is like, as 'epistemically transformative'. This is detailed in her book *Transformative Experience*, Oxford: Oxford University Press.

29. Prime Minister's Questions is held weekly (on Wednesdays at midday) in the chamber of the House of Commons. The prime minister takes questions from backbench MPs from all parties in addition to the leaders of opposition parties. The main event of the session is the questioning of the prime minister by the leader of the opposition. I recommend that any readers unfamiliar with PMQs acquaint themselves with its best (or worst, depending on one's point of view) excesses via YouTube.

30. It might be seen as somewhat ironic that Corbyn has gained this reputation as the anti-professional politician, given that his primary source of income for almost his entire working life has been politics. However, I would argue that he is a career politician, not a professional one, in the sense that he lacks the requisite experience of the latter but has shown the longevity necessary for the former.

31. Luke Blaxill and Kaspar Beelen (2016), 'A Feminized Language of Democracy? The Representation of Women at Westminster since 1945', *20th Century British History*, 27(3): pp. 412–49.

32. To be clear, current evidence on this is mixed but does seem to tend towards the view that there is something behind the argument.

33. See, for example, Harold D. Clarke, David Sanders, Marianne C. Stewart, and Paul Whiteley (2010), 'Valence Politics and Electoral Choice in Britain', *Journal of Elections, Public Opinion and Parties* 21(2): pp. 237–53. The existence of these effects is empirically disputed, however; see, for example, Geoffrey Evans and Kat Chzhen (2016), 'Re-evaluating the valence model of political choice', *Political Science Research and Methods* 4(1): pp. 199–220.

34. Andrew Gamble (2000), *Politics and Fate*, Cambridge: Polity, p. 96.

35. The American philosopher John Dewey (1927), in his book *The Public and Its Problems*, New York: Henry Holt & Co., covers similar ground, lamenting the idea that politics could be reduced to technocratic management.

36. Sandel (2010), p. 190.

37. Hélène Landemore (2013), *Democratic Reason*, Princeton, NJ: Princeton University Press, p. 110.

38. In this chapter, I will discuss broad responses in a more abstract way. In Chapter 4, having established the principles I think should govern our response, I offer a more specific set of suggestions that includes policy recommendations. The fact that many political decisions lie outside of the manifesto platforms on which parties present themselves to the electorate when it is time to vote would also be a reason to emphasize the importance of *who* is present in the assembly.

39. Landemore (2013); Jacques Rancière (2014), *Hatred of Democracy*, London: Verso.

40. Jason Brennan (2016) attacks some of these ideas, which he refers to as 'semiotic arguments for democracy', in *Against Democracy*, Princeton, NJ: Princeton University Press, p. 113.

41. Jane Suiter and her colleagues examine the Irish pilot Citizens' Assembly and find, foreshadowing the discussion below, that heterogeneous groups improve the quality of deliberation undertaken. For more, see Jane Suiter, David M. Farrell, and Eoin O'Malley (2016), 'When do deliberative citizens change their opinions? Evidence from the Irish Citizens' Assembly', *International Political Science Review*, 37(2): pp. 198–212. For discussion of the British Columbia case, see Mark E. Warren and Hilary Pearse (2008), *Designing Deliberative Democracy: The British Columbia Citizens' Assembly*, Cambridge: Cambridge University Press, p. 252. Readers can find information about citizens' juries on environmental issues in Australia in Robert E. Goodin and Simon J. Niemeyer (2003), 'When Does Deliberation Begin? Internal Reflection versus Public Discussion in Deliberative Democracy', *Political Studies* 51(4): pp. 627–49.

42. http://www.britishelectionstudy.com/custom/uploads/2015/11/BES-questionnaire-and-showcards.pdf.

43. One objection might be that there is another domain of 'political skill' or 'political acumen' that could be relevant to political decision-making. This is the notion that certain individuals, such as Lyndon Baines Johnson or Barack Obama for example, are talented at politics in a sense usually referring to the ability to gain the support and agreement of others. This might be true, though it is hard to see this as distinct in any way from a wider set of social skills that have no special relationship to politics. Even if it was true, and was unique to politics in some sense, I would argue that the relevance of these skills to politics is simply an artefact of the way political institutions are currently designed and doesn't reflect any deep foundational characteristic.

44. Landemore (2013), p. 200.

45. Recall Brennan's (2016), p. 17, anti-authority tenet: 'When some citizens are morally unreasonable, ignorant, or incompetent about politics, this justifies not permitting them to exercise political authority over others. It justifies either forbidding them from holding power or reducing the power they have in order to protect innocent people from their incompetence.'

46. Brennan (2016), p. 228.

47. Brennan (2016), ch. 9. I discuss further questions around the nature of what politics is later in this chapter.

48. Landemore (2013), p. 203.

49. Lu Hong and Scott E. Page (2004), 'Groups of diverse problem-solvers can outperform groups of high-ability problem solvers', *Proceedings of the National Academy of Sciences* vol. 101, no. 46: pp. 16385–9.

50. Hong and Page (2004), p. 16385.
51. Scott E. Page (2007), *The Difference: How the Power of Diversity Creates Better Groups, Firms, Schools, and Societies*, Princeton, NJ: Princeton University Press, p. 7.
52. The obvious question this raises is: which 'kinds' are relevant here? I will discuss this more in Chapter 4 where I suggest that it is extremely difficult, and in many ways problematic, to try and identify relevance ahead of time. I outline what seems to be the optimal solution to this issue there.
53. Page (2007), p. 10. Page continues: 'This result relies on four conditions: (1) The problem must be difficult; (2) the perspectives and heuristics that the problem solvers possess must be diverse; (3) the set of problem solvers from which we choose our collections must be large; and (4) the collections of problem solvers must not be too small.' I think the nature of political problems, the diversity inherent in the UK (or any country's) population as a whole, as well as the relative size of the population and the legislature means that these ideas apply to the generalized case of representative democracy.
54. Landemore (2013), p. 161. Very briefly, the *Diversity Prediction Theorem* relies on the fact that when we take an average of a group's predictions regarding some outcome, the overall error of their prediction is equal to the average error made by each individual predictor minus the average distance between each prediction and the overall prediction, something Page refers to as 'predictive diversity'. The upshot of this is that 'increasing prediction diversity by one unit results in the same reduction in collective error as does increasing average ability by one unit'. Leading on from this, the *Crowds Beat Averages Law* dictates that the accuracy of the collective prediction of a group can be no worse than the average accuracy of its members—'the group necessarily predicts more accurately than its average member'. Indeed, the more diverse the group becomes, the amount that it predicts better than the average member increases. Across both, what we see is that diversity improves the predictive outcomes of groups as much as increasing the average predictive ability of individual members. In other words, the requirement is not to select the 'best' predictors, but rather to select a sufficiently diverse group of them.
55. This definition is necessarily a great simplification of many works in political theory.
56. Landemore (2013), p. 97.
57. Landemore (2013), p. 92.
58. Landemore (2013), p. 92. This might be familiar to readers as the idea of the philosopher Jürgen Habermas, sometimes referred to as a 'Habermasian ideal'.
59. The full definition from Landemore and Page (2015), p. 243, is: 'Disagreement resulted from a deliberation in which people exchanged reasons that led them to update their predictions or predictive models so as to increase the accuracy of these predictions or models while preserving

their diversity (i.e. the negative correlations between the different predictions or models).' Hélène Landemore and Scott E. Page (2015), 'Deliberation and disagreement: Problem solving, prediction, and positive dissensus', *Politics, Philosophy & Economics* 14(3): pp. 229–54.

60. Deliberation has also consistently been found to increase levels of political knowledge and understanding, as well as to increase individuals' sense of their own political abilities. For a recent review see Suiter at al. (2016), and for a theoretically driven consideration see Robert C. Luskin, James S. Fishkin, and Roger Jowell (2002), 'Considered Opinions: Deliberative Polling in Britain', *British Journal of Political Science* 32: pp. 455–87.

61. Page (2007), p. 14.

62. Landemore (2013), p. 219.

63. Russell Muirhead (2014), 'The Politics of Getting It Right', *Critical Review* 26(1–2), pp. 115–28: p. 119.

64. Stephen G. W. Stich (2014), 'When Democracy Means Pluralism: Landemore's Epistemic Argument for Democracy and the Problem of Value Diversity', *Critical Review* 26(1–2), pp. 170–83: p. 175. The key point here is that, say, one of two deliberators may have reached what they feel are local optima and, incorrectly, ignore the argument from their partner, who has correctly identified some improved local optima (which in turn will overall be closer to the global optima). See Stich (2014), pp. 175–6, for more.

65. Stich (2014), p. 177.

66. Alfred Moore (2014), 'Democratic Reason, Democratic Faith, and the Problem of Expertise', *Critical Review* 26(1–2), pp. 101–14: p.113.

67. Matt Sleat (2016), 'What Is a Political Value? Political Philosophy and Fidelity to Reality', *Social Philosophy & Policy* 33(1–2), pp. 252–72: p.256.

68. Paul Gunn (2014), 'Democracy and Epistocracy', *Critical Review* 26(1–2): pp. 59–79: p.59.

69. Gunn (2014), p. 76.

70. An aside here is that even if we assume that the evidence is correct, and voters are poorly informed, this ignorance should not be taken to be something intrinsic to them.

71. See Paul Bloom (2016), *Against Empathy: The Case for Rational Compassion*, New York: HarperCollins, pp. 27–30, for discussion on this point.

72. For more on this point, see Thomas Christiano (2008), *The Constitution of Equality: Democratic Authority and Its Limits*, Oxford: Oxford University Press, especially chapter 7.

CHAPTER 4

1. One possible reform I do not consider in this chapter, or in the rest of the book, is electoral reform. This is for a number of reasons. First, evidence as to whether electoral reforms actually aid the selection and election of a

more diverse group of politicians is mixed. It is clear that the numbers of women, for example, increase in polities using non-majoritarian electoral systems, but the role of norms inside both political institutions and political parties has also been shown to be crucially important in sustaining this link. Electoral systems can be manipulated in the pursuit of inegalitarian ends, should the political will to do this exist. Second, and related, electoral reform arguably is focused more on diversity of ideas, not presence.

2. Though, as I mentioned in the previous chapter, they might.

3. Joni Lovenduski (2016) has written a robust defence of the supply-and-demand framework: 'The Supply and Demand Framework: Some Reflections', *Government & Opposition* 51(3): pp. 513–28.

4. This is taken from the title of Michael Rush's (1994) paper of the same name—'Career Patterns in British Politics: First Choose Your Party...', *Parliamentary Affairs* 47(4): pp. 566–82.

5. Adapted from Sarah Childs, Joni Lovenduski, and Rosie Campbell (2005), *Women at the Top 2005: Changing Numbers, Changing Politics?*, London: Hansard Society, p. 24.

6. http://www.theguardian.com/politics/2005/dec/06/toryleadership2005.conservatives3.

7. http://www.politics.co.uk/comment-analysis/2012/06/28/ed-miliband-unite-speech-in-full.

8. Agnès Alexandre-Collier (2016), 'The "Open Garden of Politics": The impact of open primaries for candidate selection in the British Conservative Party', *British Journal of Politics and International Relations* 18(3), pp. 706–23: p. 1. Alexandre-Collier also notes that although the Conservative primaries have been referred to as 'open', they are actually 'mixed primaries' including both party members in the constituency and registered voters (2016, p. 2).

9. Alexandre-Collier (2016), p. 9.

10. These examples are from the Conservative Party, as studied by Sarah Childs and Paul Webb (2012), *Sex, Gender and the Conservative Party: From Iron Lady to Kitten Heels*, Basingstoke: Palgrave Macmillan, p. 79.

11. Michael Hill (2013), 'Arrogant Posh Boys? The Social Composition of the Parliamentary Conservative Party and the Effect of Cameron's "A" List', *Political Quarterly* 84(1), pp. 80–9: p. 88.

12. David E. Broockman (2014), 'Mobilizing Candidates: Political Actors Strategically Shape the Candidate Pool with Personal Appeals', *Journal of Experimental Political Science* 1(2), pp. 104–19: p. 109.

13. Mona Lena Krook (2009), *Quotas for Women Worldwide*, New York: Oxford University Press; Alli Mari Tripp and Alice Kang (2007), 'The Global Impact of Quotas: On the Fast Track to Increased Female Legislative Representation', *Comparative Political Studies* 41(3): pp. 338–61.

14. Schwindt-Bayer (2009).

15. Note here that I use the term 'sex quota', which is arguably a more accurate description of what 'gender quotas' are focused on, with sex being a

biological category, gender being a socially derived one. There are a number of debates which I fully expect to arise in due course in those cases where the biological sex and chosen gender of an aspirant candidate are not necessarily in perfect alignment. In such cases, the technicalities and specifics of the policy wording might either solve the issue quickly, or remain open for interpretation.

16. To be clear, this is separate from the debate I mentioned in Chapter 3 about which characteristics might be considered politically relevant in the first place.

17. Elizabeth S. Anderson (2008), 'Expanding the Egalitarian Toolbox: Equality and Bureaucracy', *Proceedings of the Aristotelian Society Supplementary Volume LXXXII*, pp. 139–60: p. 157.

18. Andrew Rehfeld (2010), 'On Quotas and Qualifications for Office', in *Political Representation*, ed. Ian Shapiro, Susan C. Stokes, Elisabeth Jean Wood, and Alexander S. Kirshner, Cambridge: Cambridge University Press, pp. 236–68.

19. There is an inherent problem with trying to get a handle on 'quality' in this context, though, given that all the measures of quality that we tend to utilize are extrapolated from what went before.

20. Rainbow Murray (2010), 'Second Among Unequals? A Study of Whether France's "Quota Women" Are Up to the Job', *Politics & Gender* 6(1): pp. 93–118.

21. Paul Bloom (2016), *Against Empathy: The Case for Rational Compassion*, New York: HarperCollins, p. 31.

22. I borrow this terminology from Holly Lawford-Smith's (2016) 'Offsetting Class Privilege', *Journal of Practical Ethics* 4(1): pp. 23–51.

23. Jeffrey Edward Green (2016), *The Shadow of Unfairness: A Plebeian Theory of Liberal Democracy*, New York: Oxford University Press. Green highlights the 'limiting parameters' of liberal democracy itself as those of remove (discussed earlier), manyness, and plutocracy. It is primarily the first and third of these that are relevant to my argument here, but Green's diagnosis is convincing, even if his prescribed solution is somewhat defeatist in my view.

24. The question of whether they really do this is a fair one. I would argue that the empirical evidence on the issue of gender quotas suggests that women are certainly not hampered in their parliamentary work but, as I discuss later, it would be remiss to say that quotas will immediately alter a long-standing culture that undoubtedly stands on a foundation of class and other privileges.

25. Michael J. Sandel (1998), *Democracy's Discontent: America in Search of a Public Philosophy*, Cambridge, MA: Harvard University Press, p. 4.

26. Sandel (1998), p. 6.

27. Sandel (1998), p. 203.

28. In his book (2010), *Justice*, London: Penguin Books, Michael J. Sandel discusses how American universities have used 'race quota' systems and

justified this with reference to the benefits for *all* students of a more diverse student body. In the time I have been writing this book, the US Supreme Court has heard another case on such affirmative action policies, *Fisher v. University of Texas at Austin* (2016). Justice Kennedy, writing the opinion of the Court, again supports this notion, referring to it as 'the University's compelling interest' (pp. 10–11) and writes that the Court supports an interpretation of the Equal Protection Clause that 'does not force universities to choose between a diverse student body and a reputation for academic excellence' (p. 16). The full opinion can be read at http://www.supremecourt.gov/opinions/15pdf/14-981_4g15.pdf.

29. Suzanne Dovi (2009), 'In Praise of Exclusion', *Journal of Politics* 71(3): pp. 1172–86.
30. Dovi (2009), p. 1173.
31. Dovi is clear that only certain kinds of exclusion are acceptable; formal exclusion in the shape of legal barriers to voting or running for office at all are not permitted on her account. For full definitions of the terms she uses, I recommend readers look at her paper in full.
32. Though this will obviously occur as people participate, and people should be proud to do so. However, the system should not be designed solely to facilitate this, nor to prioritize it ahead of all other possible concerns.
33. Anne Phillips (2004), 'Defending Equality of Outcome', *Journal of Political Philosophy*, 12(1): pp. 1–19.
34. Martha Nussbaum (2000), 'The Costs of Tragedy: Some Moral Limits of Cost-Benefit Analysis', *Journal of Legal Studies* 29(2): p. 1007.
35. For the sake of the example, let us assume that Angela lives in a safe electoral seat and is more or less guaranteed to win if she runs.
36. Nussbaum (2000), p. 1014.
37. Of course, some groups take on greater responsibility than others in this regard. Women continue to be responsible for the majority of domestic labour, for example.
38. Nussbaum (2000), p. 1015.
39. This section draws in part on Peter Allen, David Cutts, and Madelaine Winn (2016), 'Understanding legislator experiences of family-friendly working practices in political institutions', *Politics & Gender* 12(3): pp. 549–72.
40. See Allen et al. (2016) for more.
41. Rosie Campbell and Philip Cowley (2014), 'The representation of women in politics, addressing the supply side: Public attitudes to job-sharing parliamentarians', *British Politics* 9(4): pp. 430–49.
42. The full report is available at http://www.bristol.ac.uk/media-library/sites/news/2016/july/20%20Jul%20Prof%20Sarah%20Childs%20The%20Good%20Parliament%20report.pdf.
43. https://inews.co.uk/opinion/comment/breastfeeding-parliament-unprofessional/.

44. Jeffrey A. French, Kevin B. Smith, John R. Alford, Adam Guck, Andrew K. Birnie, and John R. Hibbing (2014), 'Cortisol and politics: Variance in voting behavior is predicted by baseline cortisol levels', *Physiology and Behavior* 133: pp. 61–7.

45. French et al. (2014), p. 65.

46. Alan S. Gerber, Gregory A. Huber, David Doherty, and Conor M. Dowling (2011), 'The Big Five Personality Traits in the Political Arena', *Annual Review of Political Science* 14: pp. 265–87.

47. Monica C. Schneider, Mirya R. Holman, Amanda B. Diekman, and Thomas McAndrew (2016), 'Power, Conflict, and Community: How Gendered Views of Political Power Influence Women's Political Ambition', *Political Psychology* 37(4): pp. 515–31.

48. Schneider et al. (2015), p. 5.

49. Crucially, though, these are also likely to be related to discriminatory gender norms woven into the fabric of society at large. In our hypothetical example where social inequalities were absent, the male–female difference might have gone the same way already—indeed, it should have to a large extent.

50. See Alexander A. Guerrero (2014), 'Against Elections: The Lottocratic Alternative', *Philosophy & Public Affairs* 42(2), pp. 135–78. I discuss more of the potential specifics of this idea later. Briefly, it seems to me that the best option would be to cast the net as wide as possible here, making the eligibility pool highly inclusive. Doing otherwise immediately reduces the force of both the normative argument and the expected epistemic benefits of random selection.

51. Hélène Landemore (2013), 'Deliberation, cognitive diversity, and democratic inclusiveness: an epistemic argument for the random selection of representatives', *Synthese* 190: pp. 1209–31, makes an archetypal case of this argument.

52. This is a slight simplification, as there is some evidence that the presence of quotas alone has effects on the perceptions of women as political leaders, for example, and can benefit the wider social standing of women in contexts where they are adopted.

53. Anderson (2008), p. 143. Anderson's argument also exposes the weakness inherent in the arguments of political theorists who rely entirely on 'process democracy' to underscore the normative case in favour of democracy as a whole. Surely there is something to the argument that the guarantees offered by processes and rules are only worth as much as they are actually able to be utilized by those they are offered to?

54. Guerrero (2014), p. 169.

55. However, as I noted when discussing Nadia Urbinati's work in Chapter 2, this is not to damn the *representative* element.

56. I think that term limits are a good idea across the board, but remain unconvinced that they would have a transformative effect on composition

if enacted in isolation. Available evidence suggests that 'term limits are unlikely to create a citizen legislature – historically turnover rates have changed greatly with little or no effect on the composition or character of the legislature', Alexander Tabarrok (1994), 'A Survey, Critique, and New Defense of Term Limits', *Cato Journal* 14(2): pp. 333–48.

57. Guerrero (2014), p. 142.
58. Guerrero (2014), p. 143. His argument also focuses on the fact that capture is more likely in a system lacking in meaningful accountability for political decision makers, in particular where the electorate is low in both relevant knowledge and information about the policies in question, and low in resources in terms of actively doing anything about any disagreements that might arise.
59. The UK is not a major offender on many of these measures, though the principles apply in different ways—for example, in terms of post-office gains.
60. Shane Frederick, George Loewenstein, and Ted O'Donoghue (2002), 'Time Discounting and Time Preference: A Critical Review', *Journal of Economic Literature* XL, pp. 351–401: p. 352.
61. For more on this specific idea, see Anthony Barnett and Peter Carty (2008), *The Athenian Option: Radical Reform for the House of Lords*, Exeter: Imprint Academic.
62. Guerrero (2014), p. 156.
63. Guerrero (2014), p. 157.
64. Keith Sutherland (2008), *A People's Parliament*, Exeter: Imprint Academic.
65. Sutherland rather hastily dismisses the possibility of a democratically elected president in place of a monarch.
66. I am indebted to one of the anonymous reviewers of the manuscript for this observation.

CONCLUSION

1. Landemore (2013), p. 111.
2. A case in point: in September 2016, UKIP elected Diane James, a woman, as the new leader of the party, though she subsequently resigned after only eighteen days in charge.
3. Richard Dawkins (2006), *The Selfish Gene*, Oxford: Oxford University Press, p. 69.
4. Read more about the Committee at http://www.parliament.uk/business/committees/committees-a-z/commons-select/political-and-constitutional-reform-committee/. It has been replaced by the Public Administration and Constitutional Affairs Committee.
5. Christopher Hitchens (2011), *Hitch-22: A Memoir*, London: Atlantic Books, p. 262.
6. http://www.nytimes.com/2016/11/06/opinion/sunday/consider-a-monarchy-america.html?_r=0; https://www.theguardian.com/commentisfree/

belief/2016/nov/10/us-election-result-donald-trump-terrific-argument-for-monarchy-the-crown.

7. https://sotonpolitics.org/2016/11/11/the-failures-of-political-science-trump-brexit-and-beyond/.

8. Of course, there is much more to political science/studies as a discipline than predicting elections but, given the prominence of this part of the discipline in the public eye, I'm not sure that this is a point much appreciated outside academia. Given this, I will use this description here.

9. The tweet was subsequently deleted but is reported in various news outlets, including https://www.theguardian.com/politics/2016/sep/18/momentum-activists-labour-jeremy-corbyn-feature.

10. https://www.psa.ac.uk/insight-plus/blog/do-academics-have-corbyn-problem.

11. http://www.newstatesman.com/politics/2013/04/where-are-all-right-wing-stand-ups.

12. This is not to discount the increasing casualization of labour in academia—the voices of this group are, not unrelatedly, heard much less frequently than those of more established colleagues.

13. Robert E. Goodin (2009), *The Oxford Handbook of Political Science*, Oxford: Oxford University Press, p. 5.

14. Joe Earle, Cahal Moran, and Zach Ward-Perkins (2016), *The Econocracy: The perils of leaving economics to the experts*, Manchester: Manchester University Press, p. 5.

15. Earle et al. (2016), p. 7.

16. https://sotonpolitics.org/2016/11/11/the-failures-of-political-science-trump-brexit-and-beyond/.

17. http://www.bsg.ox.ac.uk/study.

18. Thanks to an anonymous reviewer for making this point especially clear.

19. David M. Estlund (2009), *Democratic Authority: A Philosophical Framework*, Princeton, NJ: Princeton University Press, p. 262.

Index